COOKING
★ WITH ★
TEXAS
GRANDMAS

COOKING
★ WITH ★
TEXAS
GRANDMAS

by AGNES FOSTER *and* AGNES POLASEK

NORTHLAND
PUBLISHING

Our thanks to Logene and Lynn Foster for their help in putting this together. We cleaned out our recipe boxes and threw in photographs for nostalgia. So this book is dedicated to our family and friends (even the young ones for later use). With love from both of us!
—Agnes Kucera Polasek & Agnes Polasek Foster

Cover: left, Agnes Polasek Foster; right, Agnes Polasek.
Frontis: Theo and Agnes Polasek on their wedding day, 1932.
Backcover: Agnes Brandl Kucera holding Agnes Foster
along with her family, 1939. (Agnes Polasek on left).
Page vi: John and Agnes Kucera.

NOTE: *All cooking temperatures in this book refer to degrees Fahrenheit.*
The use of trade names does not imply an endorsement by the product manufacturer.

The text type was set in Dante MT
The display type was set in Rosewood Fill
Composed in the United States of America
Designed by Mike Russell
Edited by Stephanie Bucholz
Production supervision by Lisa Brownfield

FIRST IMPRESSION
ISBN 0-87358-757-X
Foster, Agnes.
Cooking with Texas grandmas / by Agnes Foster and Agnes Polasek.
p. cm.
ISBN 0-87358-757-x (alk. paper)
1. Cookery, American–Southwestern style. 2. Cookery–Texas. I. Polasek, Agnes. II.
Title.
TX715.2.S69 F67 2000
641.59764–dc21   99-053401

CONTENTS

*Of the many recipes handed down by the authors' family, and
shared by extended family and friends over the years,
these are their favorites.*

❦

APPETIZERS, DIPS, & SNACKS

★

Agnes Kucera (Polasek), 1914.

CHEESE STRAWS

★

2 cups grated sharp Cheddar cheese

1 cup (2 sticks) butter, softened

¼ teaspoon garlic salt

¼ teaspoon salt

⅛ teaspoon ground red pepper

¼ teaspoon Worcestershire sauce

2 cups flour

2 cups crisp rice cereal

Preheat oven to 325 degrees. ★ Cream the cheese and butter until fluffy. Add seasonings. Turn electric mixer to low and add flour. Fold in cereal. Shape into very small balls and flatten with your hand. Place on ungreased cookie sheets and bake for about 10 minutes or until golden brown. DO NOT OVERCOOK. Cool thoroughly on wire racks and layer in airtight freezer container. Delicious served frozen. Can also be reheated or served at room temperature.
(MAKES ABOUT 50)

CHEESE ROLL

★

½ pound Velveeta cheese

½ pound sharp Old English cheese

1 (3-ounce) package cream cheese
  Dash garlic salt

1 clove garlic, minced

½ cup your favorite nuts (chopped fine)

1 teaspoon Lea & Perrins Worcestershire Sauce

½ (3-ounce) bottle chili powder

Mix all ingredients except chili powder and shape into a roll. Roll in chili powder.
(SERVE WITH CRACKERS)

SUPER-DELICIOUS CRAB-STUFFED EGGS
★

8 hard-boiled eggs

1 (6-ounce) can of crab meat

1 tablespoon Spanish olive oil

Salt and pepper to taste

Dash of cumin or curry powder

1 tablespoon mayonnaise

Pimiento slivers and very finely
minced parsley for garnish

Slice hard-boiled eggs sideways; remove yolks and set aside. Flake and mince the crab meat; add Spanish olive oil, salt, pepper, and cumin or curry powder. To this mixture add the egg yolks, blend well, then stir in mayonnaise. Fill the egg whites with the mixture. Over each, for garnish, lay slivers of pimiento. Border with parsley. *Deviled eggs make a super-delicious appetizer when a bit of crab meat is used in the stuffing.* (SERVES 4)

PARTY CRAB PUFFS
★

FILLING

2 (6-ounce) packages frozen
Alaskan king crab, or 2
(7½-ounce) cans crab meat

1 cup finely shredded Swiss cheese

¼ cup minced celery

2 egg yolks

BATTER

1 egg

¼ cup milk

½ cup pancake mix

SAUCE

1 (8-ounce) can tomato sauce

Combine all ingredients for filling. Form into 1-inch balls; place on waxed paper–covered baking sheets and chill at least 2 hours. ★ Beat batter ingredients together until smooth. With slotted spoon, dip crab balls, a few at a time, into batter. Deep-fry balls in corn oil over medium heat; drain on paper towels. Heat tomato sauce; use as dip for crab balls. (MAKES ABOUT 2 DOZEN)

SHRIMP OVER RITZ CRACKERS

★

WHITE SAUCE

½ stick butter

5 tablespoons flour

2 to 3 cups milk or more

SHRIMP

½ cup catsup

1 tablespoon chili powder

1 pound small, boiled shrimp, or larger, cut up into small pieces

Make the white sauce. Melt butter in skillet *(watch very carefully so it doesn't burn)*. Add flour and continue stirring until it starts to brown slightly. Immediately add 2 to 3 cups milk or more. (Use your judgment. Add more milk if you think it is too thick. Should not be watery but just thick enough to spoon on top of crackers.) Continue stirring until it is smooth. Turn fire down very low. ★ Mix catsup and chili powder together and add to white sauce. Mix together and add shrimp. Then it is ready to be served. ★ *We eat this with Ritz crackers and I make a salad to go along with it to make a meal. This was on the menu when Grandma Kucera had Logene and Agnes Foster's rehearsal dinner back in 1959. That is where I got the recipe.* (MAKES ABOUT 4 OR 5 CUPS)

Louis and Anna Polasek's family on their farm at Latium, Texas, 1900s.

GUACAMOLE DIP

★

1 cup peeled and chopped
fresh tomato

2 ripe, medium avocados, diced

1 tablespoon chopped fresh onion

2 teaspoons fresh lemon juice

1 tablespoon mayonnaise

1 teaspoon salad or olive oil

½ teaspoon Worcestershire sauce

½ teaspoon salt

¹⁄₁₆ teaspoon ground white pepper

Combine all ingredients; mix well. *(MAKES ABOUT 2 CUPS)*

HOT BROCCOLI DIP

★

3 tablespoons butter

½ cup chopped onion

½ cup chopped celery

½ cup chopped mushrooms

1 (10-ounce box or 2-pound bag)
frozen chopped broccoli, cooked
and drained

1 can condensed cream of
mushroom soup

6 ounces Velveeta cheese

¼ teaspoon garlic powder

1 teaspoon lemon juice

Sauté onion, celery, and mushrooms in butter. Add broccoli. Mix in soup, cheese, and garlic powder. Cook until cheese is melted. Add lemon juice. *(MAKES 4 CUPS)*

CHEESE DIP

★

1 (2-pound) box Velveeta cheese

1 (3-ounce) package Philadelphia cream cheese (optional)

2 (10-ounce) cans of Rotel Mexican-style diced tomatoes with lime juice and cilantro

Place all ingredients in a microwave dish and cook until melted. Serve with tortilla chips. (MAKES ABOUT 6 CUPS)

CRAB MEAT DIP

★

1 can crab meat

1 cup sour cream

½ teaspoon salt

½ teaspoon horseradish dash or 2 teaspoons Tabasco sauce

Blend all ingredients together. Serve on crackers. (MAKES ABOUT 2 CUPS)

CREAMY DILL DIP

★

1 cup Kraft Real Mayonnaise

2 tablespoons finely chopped onion

1 tablespoon milk

1 tablespoon fresh chopped dill (or 1 teaspoon dried)

Combine ingredients; mix well. Chill. Serve with vegetable dippers. (MAKES 1 CUP)

SHRIMP COCKTAIL DIP

★

Juice of 1 lemon

1 (8-ounce) package cream cheese

1 (8-ounce) jar cocktail sauce

Blend all ingredients together. Use shrimp, carrot sticks, or chips to dip. (MAKES 2 CUPS)

OYSTER CRACKER SNACKS

★

2 (10-ounce) packages oyster crackers

1 package Hidden Valley Ranch Dip Mix or Ranch Salad Dressing Mix

1½ cups corn oil

1½ tablespoons dill weed

1½ teaspoons lemon pepper

Preheat oven to 200 degrees. ★ Mix all ingredients in an oven-proof dish. Heat for 1 hour. Stir every 15 minutes. (MAKES ABOUT 8 CUPS)

Agnes & Simon Brandl, East Bernard, Texas early 1900s.
Agnes Polasek's maternal grandparents.

STUFFED MUSHROOMS

★

50 fresh mushrooms (about three 8-
   ounce containers)

3 tablespoons butter

½ cup finely chopped onion

6 green onions, finely chopped

3 garlic cloves, minced

1 (3-ounce) package cream cheese,
   softened

1½ cups soft bread crumbs
   (about 4 pieces of bread)

Salt and pepper to taste

Remove stems from cleaned mushrooms and chop stems finely in food proces-sor. Do not purée. Scrape out the insides of mushroom caps with the tip of a potato peeler or spoon and add to chopped stems. ★ Melt butter in large sauté pan over medium heat. Sauté onion, garlic, and chopped mushroom stems until most of the liquid has evaporated from the mushrooms, about 10 to 15 minutes. Stir in cream cheese. Add bread crumbs. Season with salt and pepper. Stir until mixture holds together well enough to form a ball. If too dry, add more butter. If too moist, add a few more bread crumbs. ★ Spoon mixture into mushroom caps; press firmly. Place on a cookie sheet. Bake at 350 degrees on top oven rack 10 to 15 minutes. Serve hot. (MAKES 50 APPETIZERS)

JUNK

★

2 cups Cheerios

1 (10-ounce) box Rice Chex

1 (10-ounce) box Wheat Chex

1 (12-ounce) box mixed nuts

1 (10-ounce) package pretzels

½ cup bacon grease (or just corn oil)

½ cup butter

1 tablespoon garlic salt

1 tablespoon Worcestershire sauce

1 tablespoon savory sauce

Mix all together in a large saucepan and cook for 1 hour at 250 degrees. (MAKES ENOUGH FOR 15 TO 20)

SOUPS & SALADS

★

Louis and Anna Polasek, early 1900s.
Agnes Polasek's mother-in-law and father-in-law.

POTATO SOUP
★

4 boiling potatoes

½ cup milk

3 slices Velveeta cheese

½ teaspoon onion powder

Salt and pepper to taste

Boil potatoes. When potatoes are really cooked soft and almost falling apart, chop into small pieces, add milk, cheese, onion powder, and salt and pepper. *(ENOUGH FOR 4)*

FAST CHICKEN NOODLE SOUP
★

1 (3- to 4-pound) fryer chicken

1 teaspoon salt

½ teaspoon pepper

½ (4-ounce) package noodles

¼ onion, whole or chopped (depending on whether your family dislikes finding onion in it)

2 packages chicken noodle cup-of-soup mix

Thoroughly wash fryer and place in large pot. Cover with water and put in salt, pepper, and onion. Cook fryer until it is almost falling off bone (about 1 hour). Then debone fryer and place meat back into pot. Add noodles and soup mix and cook about 10 minutes. It is ready to eat. *(ENOUGH FOR 8)*

HEARTY FISH CHOWDER

★

1½ pounds fish fillets

5 slices bacon

2 cloves garlic, finely chopped

1 (28-ounce) can stewed tomatoes

2 (8-ounce) cans tomato sauce

2 cups O'Brien potatoes (or any
    potato mix)

¼ teaspoon thyme

1 teaspoon hot pepper sauce

¼ cup soy sauce

2 cups water

½ cup dry vermouth

Chopped fresh parsley for garnish

Cut fish into 1-inch pieces and set aside. Fry bacon until crisp, reserving bacon drippings. Crumble bacon and set aside. Cook garlic in reserved bacon drippings until tender. Add all remaining ingredients together except vermouth and parsley. Cover and simmer for 30 minutes. Stir in vermouth. Sprinkle each serving with fresh parsley. Serve with crusty bread. *(MAKES 6 SERVINGS)*

CRANBERRY BEAUTY SALAD

★

1 pound fresh cranberries

2 cups sugar

2 cups seedless grapes

1 cup chopped pecans

2 cups miniature marshmallows

1 cup heavy cream, whipped, or 2
    cups frozen whipped topping,
    thawed

Wash and drain cranberries. Grind in food chopper using coarse blade (or use a blender). Add sugar and refrigerate over-night or at least 4 hours. Add grapes, pecans, and marshmallows. Fold in whipped cream. Refrigerate until serving. *(MAKES ENOUGH FOR ABOUT 10)*

Simon and Agnes Brandl's farm in East Bernard, Texas.
left—Agnes Brandl Kucera, right—Augusta Brandl Schulzer.

CHERRY COKE SALAD

★

1 (16-ounce) can pitted bing
  cherries, liquid reserved

1 (8-ounce) can crushed
  pineapple, liquid reserved

2 (3-ounce) packages cherry-
  flavored gelatin

16 ounces Coca Cola (not too cold)

1 cup pecans, chopped

Drain juice from cherries and pineapple to yield 2 cups of liquid (or add water
to make 2 cups). Heat the liquid to almost boiling point. Add gelatin and stir
until dissolved. Add Coca Cola. Put in refrigerator and when partly congealed,
add cherries, pineapple, and chopped nuts. (Stir slightly to mix.) *Looks really
good in a pretty mold.* (MAKES ENOUGH FOR 10 PEOPLE)

CRANBERRY-CREAM GELATIN SALAD

★

1 (3-ounce) package cherry-
  flavored gelatin

1 cup hot water

1 (16-ounce) can whole berry
  cranberry sauce

½ cup diced celery

¼ cup chopped walnuts

1 cup sour cream

Salad greens for garnish

Dissolve gelatin in hot water. Chill until thickened, but not firm. Break up
cranberry sauce with a fork. Stir sauce, celery, and nuts into gelatin mixture.
Fold in sour cream. Pour in 1-quart mold and chill until firm. Place pretty
lettuce leaves or other greens on plate. Unmold salad on greens.
(MAKES 4 TO 6 SERVINGS)

REGAL CRAB MEAT SALAD

★

2 (6½-ounce) cans crab meat, or 1 (12-ounce) package fresh or frozen shrimp (2 cups)

2 cups rice, cooked and cooled

1 (8-ounce) can green peas, drained

1½ cups finely chopped celery

¼ cup sliced pimientos

1 cup mayonnaise

1½ tablespoons lemon juice

1 teaspoon salt

¼ teaspoon pepper

¼ cup sliced black olives (optional)

Lettuce cups for serving

Tomato wedges for garnish

Combine crab meat or shrimp, rice, peas, celery, and pimientos. Blend remaining ingredients and pour over crab meat mixture. Toss lightly. Adjust seasonings if necessary, chill and serve in lettuce cups. Garnish with tomato wedges if desired.
(MAKES 6 SERVINGS)

POTATO SALAD

★

4 cups cooked or baked potatoes, chopped into ½-inch cubes

2 tablespoons vinegar

1 teaspoon chopped parsley

2 eggs, boiled and cut into small pieces

1 cup yogurt

½ cup mayonnaise

Mix all together and chill about 1 hour.
(MAKES ENOUGH FOR 4 PEOPLE)

John Kucera (Czech Army 1906).
Agnes Polasek's father before he came to America.

CHRISTMAS SALAD

★

½ cup sliced almonds

5 tablespoons sugar

½ head iceberg lettuce

½ head romaine or other green leafy
   lettuce

1 cup chopped celery

2 whole green onions, chopped

¼ cup vegetable oil

1 tablespoon chopped parsley

2 tablespoons vinegar

Dash Tabasco sauce

½ teaspoon salt

Dash pepper

1 (11-ounce) can mandarin
   oranges, drained

Cook almonds in 3 tablespoons of the sugar until sugar dissolves. Cool and put in a container and refrigerate. Tear up lettuce, place in bag, and refrigerate. Chop up celery and green onions, bag, and refrigerate. Put the remaining ingredients except for mandarin oranges together in another bag or container and refrigerate. The next day you just throw it all together and add oranges. *You don't have to do the day before but it is much simpler.* (MAKES ENOUGH FOR 8 OR 10 PEOPLE)

LIGHT-STYLE GREEN GODDESS DRESSING

★

⅓ cup fresh parsley leaves

2 tablespoons white vinegar

2 cloves garlic

1 tablespoon sugar

½ teaspoon dried tarragon

½ teaspoon salt

2 cups plain yogurt

In electric blender, combine parsley, vinegar, garlic, sugar, tarragon, and salt. Whirl until finely puréed. Stir (don't use blender) into yogurt.
(MAKES ABOUT 2½ CUPS)

DINNERS

★

Theo Otto Polasek, 1928.

POULTRY

*YOU CAN BROIL IT, FRY IT, BAKE IT,
DO SHISH KEBABS, OR USE IT IN CASSEROLES.*

FRIED CHICKEN

★

We like chicken washed thoroughly, cut in pieces, salted and peppered, and rolled in plain flour (white or wheat). Then fry in a skillet with about ½ inch corn oil. We start it covered and after you turn it one time, take the lid off and finish frying without the lid for really crispy chicken. Sometimes we dip chicken into egg and then flour before frying but we really prefer plain flour most of the time. There are a lot of recipes out there with batter that make a thicker crust. It is just a matter of preference

BROILED CHICKEN

★

Salt and pepper thoroughly washed chicken and cut it up (or buy chicken parts from grocery store or in large quantities from wholesale places—this is what I like to do). If you are going to do a lot of chicken, only cut the fryers in half because they are easier to handle. Salt and pepper chicken and place on charcoal grill. After first side starts to brown, turn it over and brush with or dip into a pan of melted butter and lemon juice. When chicken is golden brown and the bone pulls out of leg easily, it is ready to eat.

SHISH KEBAB

★

Marinate chunks of chicken meat (or beef) in Wishbone Italian dressing for 2 hours or more and lace onto skewers along with fresh mushrooms, squash chunks, small tomatoes, corn on the cob (cut in small chunks), or any other vegetable you like. Grill over hot coals 10 to 15 minutes or until chicken is no longer pink inside.

CHICKEN AND DUMPLINGS

★

CHICKEN

1-3-or 4-pound fryer

Salt and pepper to taste

1 tablespoon onion powder

½ onion

DUMPLINGS

3 cups Bisquick All-Purpose Baking Mix

1 cup milk

1 or 2 envelopes chicken cup-of-soup mix (optional)

Place washed fryer in a big pot of boiling water. Add salt, pepper, onion powder, and onion. Cook until chicken starts to come off bone. Take fryer out, let cool, and debone. ★ Make your Bisquick dumplings. Mix Bisquick and milk and dump by spoonfuls into boiling chicken broth. Lower fire and cook, uncovered, for 10 minutes. Put deboned chicken (tear up pieces of chicken by hand or chop coarsely) into broth and dumplings. Try not to mix too much. Go lightly. Cook 10 minutes more, covered. If it doesn't have the taste you like you can add an envelope or two of cup of chicken soup mix. (*SERVES 2 TO 8 PEOPLE*)

KING RANCH CHICKEN

★

4 dozen corn tortillas

12 cups cooked chicken (four 4-pound fryers)

4 pounds Cheddar cheese, shredded

5 (10¾-ounce) cans cream of mushroom soup

3 (28-ounce) or 6 (10-ounce) cans Rotel tomatoes, including liquid

Pepper to taste

Garlic salt to taste

2 cups chicken broth

Tear tortillas into pieces (makes serving easier). Cover the bottoms of four 9 x 13-inch shallow baking pans with some tortillas pieces. Layer chicken, cheese (reserving some to sprinkle on the top), tomatoes, soup, tortillas, pepper, and garlic salt in pans. Sprinkle top with layers of cheese. Cover and refrigerate if preparing the day before. Add ½ chicken broth to each pan just before baking. Bake at 350 degrees for 45 minutes. (*SERVES ABOUT 25 OR 30 PEOPLE*)

CHICKEN ENCHILADAS

★

½ stick butter

1½ cups chopped onion

2 (10-ounce) cans Rotel tomatoes,
　drained, liquid reserved

1 (28-ounce) can tomatoes,
　drained, liquid reserved

1 (2-pound) box Velveeta cheese,
　cut into chunks

1 (4-pound) fryer, cooked,
　deboned, and cut into pieces

30 corn tortillas

2 cups sour cream

Sauté onion in butter. Add drained tomatoes and let cook down. Add cheese, stirring occasionally as it melts. Then add chicken to mixture. Should be thick. Add some of the tomato liquid if necessary. Take a skillet and rub butter on it and place one tortilla on it at a time. When each is heated, place in two 9 x 13-inch dishes or one large baking dish. Fill each tortilla with chicken and cheese mixture and roll up like an enchilada. Repeat this in skillet with each tortilla and when baking dish is filled up, pour the rest of the chicken mixture on top. Top with sour cream in daubs. Bake at 350 degrees for 30 minutes.
(SERVES ABOUT 15 PEOPLE)

TURKEY (OR LARGE HEN) AND DRESSING

★

Turkey (whatever size you desire)

Salt and pepper to taste

Onion powder (just sprinkle on)

Preheat oven to 350 degrees. ★ *Mother likes to cook her turkey in a covered roaster. I like to cook mine in a large turkey cooking bag.* In either case, wash bird thoroughly and salt and pepper and sprinkle some onion powder on the turkey (both inside and out). If using a bag, put a few tiny holes in the top. If using a roaster, spray Pam on roaster and place bird in pan. Stuff with dressing (using Bread Dressing or Corn Bread Dressing, opposite) and put lid on turkey or tie bag. Place in oven. Refer to chart on page 140 for how long to roast according to how much your stuffed turkey weighs.

BREAD DRESSING

★

3 cups homemade bread or
  hamburger buns, toasted and
  crumbled

1 stick butter

½ cup chopped onion

½ cup chopped celery

1 cup cooked, chopped chicken
  meat or turkey

3 eggs, beaten

1 cup chicken broth

Preheat oven to 350 degrees. Sauté onion and celery in butter until soft. Cool. Put bread crumbs in a bowl. Add chicken and eggs. Add 1 cup chicken broth. Mix together; should be soft. Put mixture over bread crumbs and mix. Everything is done so just bake until browned. Just double or triple to make more. (*MAKES ENOUGH FOR ABOUT 10 PEOPLE*)

CORN BREAD DRESSING

★

2 packages Yellow Corn Bread Mix,
  or double Golden Corn Bread
  recipe on page 58

5 slices bread (preferably homemade bread but can use about
  2½ hot dog or hamburger buns)

½ chopped onion

Salt and pepper to taste

Celery powder or celery seed to taste

2 or 3 cans chicken broth

Make a double batch of corn bread. After corn bread is cooked and cooled, crush it up in a bowl. Take the bread or buns and hold them under the faucet with warm water running. Then squeeze the water out and put the bread into the bowl with corn bread. Also put in chopped onion, salt and pepper, and celery powder. Put in chicken broth one can at a time. It's just right when you can barely pick up and place in turkey. Mix all of this very well and then taste to see if it needs anything else. Place in a baking dish that has been sprayed with Pam so that mixture is about 1½ inches high or place in the turkey. Place in oven and bake for about 30 minutes if in a pan by itself. (*MAKES ENOUGH FOR ABOUT 10 PEOPLE*)

GIBLET GRAVY

★

⅛ inch corn oil in skillet   2 or 3 cans chicken broth

⅛ onion, chopped   Cooked turkey giblets, chopped

5 tablespoons flour

Sauté onion in oil. Add flour and stir until it starts to turn brown (not long and don't let it burn) and add cans of chicken broth just as you might use water in other gravy recipes. Open 1 can of broth at a time. If you have any juice from cooking turkey, you can use that instead of canned chicken broth. Just keep stirring the mixture and adding broth and water as needed until it is the right consistency. Stir it and as it gets thick, just add more broth until it remains right. Then add salt and pepper to taste. (If you use broth from the turkey, it will already have some seasoning, so be sure to taste it before adding salt and pepper.) Then add the cooked giblets that have been chopped up. *What I do is buy a package of gizzards at the store and also use the ones out of turkey. Just boil these until they are tender and as they are cooking, add salt, pepper, and a slice of onion for taste.* (MAKES ENOUGH FOR ABOUT 8 PEOPLE)

Men playing Taroks, a Czech card game, in Hungerford, Texas, around 1920.

EGGS

You can boil eggs, fry eggs, scramble eggs, poach eggs, make quiche, deviled eggs, or use them in casseroles. Always use a coated skillet with eggs.

FRIED EGGS

★

If you use a skillet with coating, you can fry the eggs without any oil or butter at all. Or, if you prefer, rub the bottom of the skillet with butter or corn oil. Place the egg or eggs in skillet and as the white of the egg starts to turn white, slip the egg over and it is done. For sunnyside up, place in skillet with a little oil (⅛ inch) and just spoon the hot oil over the top of the egg. Cook to your desired consistency.

SCRAMBLED EGGS

★

Beat several (I use 2 per person) eggs lightly with a fork. Add ½ tablespoon of water for each egg (you can use milk or cream but water makes them fluffier). I like to add cheese and picante sauce also (depending who is here to eat it) while others like to add onion, ham bits, bacon bits, etc. Pour into a skillet in which you have melted 1 tablespoon butter over low heat. When edges thicken, stir gently and repeat until done (not real done— eggs will keep cooking a little after taken off fire). Add salt and pepper if you like. Serve while still moist. If you want to make an omelet, use 3 eggs per person and pour that amount of beaten up eggs, water, and seasoning into center of skillet and let cook a little more and then turn whole thing over and put whatever you want on top of your omelet, fold over and flip again. I like to use bacon or ham pieces, mushrooms, and slices of Velveeta cheese.

BOILED EGGS

★

Three-minute eggs mean just that. Put the eggs in a pot of cold water, boil for 3 minutes, then take out and drain off water. The egg will continue to cook a little as it sits so if you want a true three-minute egg you should try to crack and peel it as soon as you can handle it. Crack shell all around and then try to peel (under cold running water) or crack around the middle with a knife, cut open, and scoop out with a spoon. ★ For hard-boiled eggs for Easter or to put in a salad cook 10 minutes or more. These you can let cool before handling. Crack shell all around so they are easy to peel under cold running water.

POACHED EGGS

★

Take a muffin tin and either rub butter in holes or spray with Pam. Break and drop one egg in each hole. Place in oven for 15 or 20 minutes at 325 degrees and cook until white is firm or however you like it. You can test the egg by putting a fork into the white for your desired consistency. ★ Another way is to use an egg poacher. Heat water, put in rack. Place small amount of butter in each cup, put in egg, cover and simmer for 3 to 5 minutes.

DEVILED EGGS

★

Set out 6 eggs, prepared mustard, vinegar, mayonnaise, paprika, and salt and pepper. Place eggs gently in saucepan. Add cold water to ½ inch above tops of eggs and cover with lid. Heat to boiling and turn fire down to very low. Cook 20 minutes. Place pan in sink. Run cold water over eggs till cool enough to handle. Tap eggs lightly all over and peel under cold running water. ★ Put eggs on cutting board. Cut each in half lengthwise. Remove yolks carefully and put in small bowl. With fork, mash yolks and add 1 teaspoon of prepared mustard, ½ teaspoon vinegar, and 3 tablespoons mayonnaise. Mix well. Spoon yolk mixture lightly into boiled egg whites. Sprinkle tops with paprika. Place eggs in a single layer in baking pan or flat dish. Cover and keep chilled in refrigerator until serving time.

QUICHE LORRAINE

★

2 cups (8 ounces) shredded Swiss
cheese

12 slices bacon, fried and crumbled

2 uncooked pie shells

2 cups milk

4 eggs, lightly beaten

2 tablespoons flour

½ teaspoon salt

Dash of pepper

2 tablespoons chopped onion

(1 tablespoon if dried)

2 tablespoons butter, melted

2 tablespoons grated Parmesan
cheese

Toss together Swiss cheese and bacon and place in bottom of uncooked pie shells. In a bowl, mix all other ingredients except butter and Parmesan. Pour over cheese mixture in pie shells (it's usually too much so place pie pan on cookie pan for spills.) Drizzle on butter and sprinkle Parmesan. Bake 40 minutes at 375 degrees. Let stand 10 minutes before serving. (MAKES 2 PIES, ABOUT 6 SLICES PER PIE)

BLENDER HOLLANDAISE SAUCE

★

3 egg yolks

2 tablespoons lemon juice

¼ teaspoon salt

½ cup hot melted butter

Blend egg yolks, lemon juice, and salt in an electric blender. Using low speed, slowly add butter. To keep warm, pour into heat-proof dish, cover, and place in a saucepan of hot water. Stir occasionally. If sauce thickens too much, add 1 to 2 teaspoons water and beat until smooth. (MAKES 1 CUP)

BEEF

*Four recipes are devoted to cooking round steak
(always a favorite of our family). These are all the ways we cook it.
Always tenderize before cooking (or buy tenderized meat).
We really like cooking round steak in a heavy, cast-iron skillet.
(If my meat is not tenderized, I just pound it with my tenderizing hammer,
or you can use the edge of a plastic saucer or heavy knife like a hammer.)*

REGULAR ROUND STEAK

★

1 round steak slab, tenderized	Flour to coat steak
Salt and pepper to taste	½ inch corn oil in skillet

Salt and pepper the round steak and cut into the size pieces you like to serve. Roll in flour and brown in skillet. Serve with any vegetable such as potatoes and squash, corn, peas, or beans. *(SERVES 6 TO 8)*

CRACKER CHICKEN-FRIED STEAK

★

1 round steak slab, tenderized	3 tablespoons milk
Salt and pepper to sprinkle	cracker crumbs to coat steak
2 eggs	½ inch corn oil in skillet

Salt and pepper round steak. Cut into the size pieces you like. Beat up two eggs and add milk. Dip steak pieces in egg batter and then in cracker crumbs. (I like to use regular saltines. Take one tube of crackers, place in a large Ziploc bag, and crush with a rolling pin. Or you can buy cracker crumbs). Then fry to golden brown in corn oil. If you don't like the cracker crumbs, you can just use flour. *(SERVES 6 TO 8)*

SIMPLE ROAST BEEF

★

1 chuck roast, any size

Salt and pepper to taste

Onion powder to taste

Roast should be at room temperature—take out of the refrigerator in the morning if making for lunch. ★ Preheat oven to 375 degrees. ★ Sprinkle salt, pepper, and sprinkle onion powder on roast. Place the roast on a rack in a shallow baking pan and put it in oven. Cook for 1 hour at 375 degrees while you get ready for the day. Then turn off the oven but do not open the oven door. (If you do, you will let out all the steam and louse up the whole process.) Allow to sit in oven 3 hours (like while you go to church). About 20 minutes before you want to serve, turn the oven back on to 300 degrees to warm. When warm, serve. This procedure even works on a frozen roast, but add 30 minutes cooking time. (A LARGE, 2-INCH CHUCK ROAST SERVES 8 TO 10 PEOPLE)

SMOTHERED ROUND STEAK

★

1 round steak slab, tenderized

Salt and pepper to taste

Flour to coat steak

½ inch corn oil in skillet

This was a favorite of Leslie and Madeline Foster—it's actually their recipe. After tenderized round steak is salted and peppered and cut into pieces, roll pieces in flour and place in skillet. Layer one on top of the other and cook, covered. After a few minutes, when you think the steak on the bottom is brown, carefully take out the meat one by one and put on a plate or on the lid, turn the bottom pieces, and place all the meat back on top. After the bottom steak is browned on the other side, take it out, rearrange, and repeat the process until all is browned. The pieces don't have to be really brown, just done. Use your judgment. Sometimes I like to add pieces of sliced onion on the steak on the platter and cover with foil to soften the onion. It gives it a good flavor. (SERVES 6 TO 8)

OVEN-SMOTHERED ROUND STEAK

★

Do the same as in Smothered Round Steak but instead of putting the cooked steak on a plate, put it in a baking dish. Make Brown Gravy (see recipe page 30), put it over the meat, and cook in oven for 30 minutes at 325 degrees. It makes the meat more tender. This is great for doing venison round steak. (SERVES 6 TO 8)

POT ROAST
(OUR FAVORITE)

★

1 pot roast, any size (I prefer chuck roast)

Salt and pepper to taste

Onion powder to taste

2 tablespoons Kitchen Bouquet Browning & Seasoning Sauce

1 onion, peeled and cut into chunks

1 (30-ounce) package carrots, peeled and sliced

5 medium Irish or white potatoes, peeled and cut in half

Use a turkey-size roasting bag. Put bag in a large pan. Salt, pepper, and sprinkle onion powder on the roast and place in bag in the pan. Drop 2 tablespoons of Kitchen Bouquet (great seasoning for cooking meat) on top of roast and spread with a spoon on the top part of the roast. Place onion, carrots, and potatoes into pot on the sides and all around roast and partially on top if necessary. Cook according to instructions on cooking chart on page 141 (depends on size of roast). ★ When the meat is done I place it on a cutting board, slice across the grain, and place it on a serving plate (something that can be put in the microwave to reheat). Also place carrots around the meat for looks. Cover with plastic wrap or foil. ★ Make Roast Gravy (recipe page 30) using water and some of the juice from the roasting bag (about half of the juice) instead of milk. Pour the rest of the juice over the meat on the plate. Put potatoes and onions in serving dish. All of this can be done ahead of time and then reheated easily. (A LARGE, 2-INCH CHUCK ROAST SERVES 8 TO 10 PEOPLE)

MEATBALLS IN GRAVY OVER RICE

★

MEATBALLS

4 pounds ground beef

Salt and pepper to taste

Onion powder to taste (about 2 teaspoons)

1 cup flour

¾ inch corn oil in skillet

GRAVY

⅛ inch corn oil in skillet

⅛ onion, chopped

5 tablespoons flour

1 (8-ounce) can tomato sauce plus water

Salt and pepper to taste

2 tablespoons Worcestershire sauce

1 teaspoon sugar

2 cups rice, cooked

Sprinkle hamburger meat with the salt, pepper, and onion powder according to taste and mix really well. Put about 1 cup of flour (you may need more) in the middle of a plate. Make meat into small balls (about 1 inch in diameter), putting them on plate as you make them and rolling them in the flour. ★ Start your skillet with about ¾ inch of corn oil. When oil is hot place meatballs in skillet (preferably not touching) and brown on both sides. While they are cooking, you can make up another plate of hamburger balls and repeat same process. After each pan of meatballs is ready, just place in a bowl until finished browning all. ★ After all meatballs are browned, empty the corn oil out and make a gravy with fresh oil. Put about 5 tablespoons of oil in skillet and brown chopped onion. As soon as onion is sautéed, add the 5 tablespoons flour, mix thoroughly and let lightly brown. Then quickly add tomato sauce and as much water as it takes to make a gravy. Just keep mixing and adding water until you get the right consistency. Then add salt and pepper to taste, Worcestershire sauce, and sugar. Then throw back in your meatballs. You are finally done. Serve this over rice along with a salad or a vegetable for a good meal.

(MAKES ABOUT 8 SERVINGS)

SWEDISH MEATBALLS

★

1 cup bread crumbs

½ cup whipping cream

2 teaspoons butter

½ cup minced onions

1 pound ground beef

1½ teaspoons salt (optional)

½ teaspoon paprika

1 egg, lightly beaten

½ teaspoon ground nutmeg

Corn oil for browning meatballs

GRAVY

1 package onion soup mix

1½ cups water

Soak crumbs in cream for ten minutes and set aside. Sauté onions in butter. Add meat and all other ingredients, including soaked crumbs, and mix well. Form balls and brown in skillet with about ¼-inch corn oil until done. ★ For gravy: Combine onion soup mix and water. Pour mixture over meatballs; cover and simmer. (MAKES ENOUGH FOR 4 PEOPLE)

SAVORY STUFFED PEPPERS

★

1 pound ground beef

¼ cup chopped onion

1 (12-ounce) can corn, drained

1 (8-ounce can) tomato sauce

1 cup cooked rice

¼ cup A-1 steak sauce

¼ teaspoon ground black pepper

6 large green bell peppers

In a skillet, over medium heat, brown meat and cook onion until done; pour off drippings. Stir in corn, tomato sauce, rice, steak sauce, and pepper; set aside. Cut tops off of bell peppers and remove seeds. Spoon meat mixture into peppers; arrange in a 9 x 9 x 2-inch baking pan. Bake at 350 degrees for 30 to 35 minutes or until peppers are done. (MAKES 6 SERVINGS)

CHEESEBURGER PIE

★

1 pound ground beef

1 cup chopped onion

½ teaspoon salt

1 cup shredded Cheddar cheese

1 cup milk

½ cup Bisquick All-Purpose Baking Mix

2 eggs

Preheat oven to 400 degrees. ★ Brown beef and onion in a skillet; drain. Stir in salt. Spread in slightly greased (or Pam-sprayed) 9-inch pie plate. Sprinkle with cheese. Combine milk, Bisquick, and eggs and stir until blended. Pour over cheese. Bake 25 minutes or until fork comes out clean when placed in mixture. *(MAKES 8 SERVINGS)*

PIZZA BURGERS

★

⅔ cup evaporated milk

1½ pounds ground chuck

½ cup cracker or bread crumbs

¼ cup finely chopped onions

1 teaspoon garlic salt

½ teaspoon salt

2 tablespoons grated Parmesan cheese

4 hamburger buns

1 cup tomato sauce

¾ teaspoon crushed oregano leaves

1 cup (4 ounces) shredded mozzarella cheese

Preheat oven to 425 degrees. ★ Combine milk, meat, crumbs, onion, garlic salt, salt, and Parmesan cheese in large mixing bowl; mix well. Split buns in half and toast lightly. Divide meat mixture into 8 parts; spread on the 8 bun halves. Place on cookie sheet. Make well in center of meat with the back of a spoon. Combine sauce and oregano. Spoon 2 tablespoons of mixture into each well. Bake for 20 minutes. Sprinkle 2 tablespoons cheese over each. Continue cooking until cheese melts. *(SERVES 4)*

WHITE GRAVY

★

⅛ inch corn oil in skillet

1 slice chopped onion (optional)

5 tablespoons flour

3 cups milk or until right consistency

Salt and pepper to taste

Sauté onion (and if somebody doesn't like onion pieces, take out now). Add flour and brown lightly. Add milk a little at a time and mix constantly until right consistency. Salt and pepper to taste. *(MAKES ABOUT 4 CUPS)*

BROWN OR ROAST GRAVY

★

Same as White Gravy only use juice from cooking roast or water instead of milk. Use a dash of Kitchen Bouquet Browning & Seasoning Sauce plus other seasonings. *(MAKES ABOUT 4 CUPS)*

WHITE SAUCE

★

½ stick butter

5 tablespoons flour

2 to 3 cups milk

Salt and pepper to taste

Melt butter in skillet and add flour. Mix and as it begins to lightly brown, add milk a little at a time until right consistency. Stir constantly. Salt and pepper to taste. *(MAKES ABOUT 3½ CUPS)*

John Kucera planting cotton, late 1920s. Agnes Polasek's father.

PORK

PORK SHOULD BE HANDLED VERY CAREFULLY. IT CAN GO BAD RATHER FAST. WHEN YOU PURCHASE IT IN THE STORE, ALWAYS PICK PORK IN A REALLY CLEAN-LOOKING CONTAINER AND ALSO SMELL IT TO SEE THAT IT HASN'T GONE BAD. YOU CAN FREEZE FRESH PORK BUT DO NOT REFREEZE. FRY PORK RIBS AND BACON RATHER DRY SO YOU DON'T GET SO MUCH FAT. PORK CHOPS AND ROASTS YOU SHOULD COOK UNTIL THE MEAT TURNS WHITE. DO NOT OVERCOOK. ON ROASTS, ETC., BE SURE TO USE A MEAT THERMOMETER. COOK TO THE TEMPERATURE ON THE CHART ON PAGE 140.

BACON
★

Fry all bacon rather crisp, particularly if you are using fresh bacon. This is one of our favorites. You have to ask the butcher to save you some fresh bacon with the rind before he smokes it. Slightly salt the bacon before putting in skillet and fry in a little corn oil until really crisp (not burned). When frying smoked bacon, also fry crisp.

PORK CHOPS
★

Do not overcook pork chops, but be sure all inside meat is white in color when you take it out of the skillet. Salt and pepper before putting in skillet. Fry in about ½ inch corn oil.

PORK ROAST
★

Use salt, pepper, and onion powder to season your pork roast. Place on a rack in a pan and cook, uncovered, until it is brown and the temperature has reached the level specified in the chart on page 140. The temperature is very important because you don't want it overcooked but with pork you very definitely want it cooked thoroughly. Place the thermometer in the thickest part of the roast.

PORK RIBS
★

Baby back ribs are the easiest to fry. They are all small and about the same size. If you get a rack of ribs, you just have to be sure to fry the thicker part a little more than the other. Salt and pepper and fry in about ½ inch of corn oil. Fry really well to get all the fat out.

SEAFOOD

CRAB DELIGHT

★

1 (8-ounce) package cream cheese

2 tablespoons mayonnaise

2 teaspoons Worcestershire sauce

½ teaspoon seasoned salt

1 cup flaked, cooked crab meat

8 (3-inch) toast rounds

8 slices tomato

8 (3-inch) round slices Cheddar cheese

Preheat oven to 350 degrees. ★ Beat first four ingredients together until light and fluffy. Stir in crab meat. Place toast rounds on baking sheet; spread crab meat mixture over toast and top each with a tomato slice and a slice of cheese. Bake about 15 minutes. *(MAKES 8 OPEN-FACED SANDWICHES)*

DEVILED CRAB

★

1 cup toasted bread crumbs or cracker crumbs

¼ to ½ stick butter

2 jars pimientos

2 or 3 eggs, beaten

Onion, celery, and green bell pepper (as much as you like), all diced

1 cup crab meat (or more)

Preheat oven to 350 degrees. Toast bread crumbs; sauté onions, celery, and bell peppers in butter. Mix together crumbs, sautéed ingredients, pimientos, eggs, and crab meat. Spray an 8 x 8-inch casserole dish with Pam and fold crab mixture into dish. Bake 30 minutes at 350 degrees. *(SERVES ABOUT 4)*

STUFFED CRAB

(OR MAY BE USED TO STUFF LARGE FLOUNDER ALSO)

★

1 stick celery, finely chopped

½ onion, finely chopped

1 green bell pepper, finely chopped, or 1 (2-ounce) jar pimiento peppers

¼ stick butter

1 can cream of mushroom soup

2 cups crab meat

1 to 1½ cups cracker crumbs

Black pepper to taste

Preheat oven to 350 degrees. ★ Sauté celery, onions, and green peppers in butter until tender but not brown. Then put in mushroom soup and crab meat. Warm well and then add cracker crumbs (enough to make the right mixture—the really fine crumbs you buy at the store are probably best for this) and pepper. Place in crab shell or in baking dish. Bake for 30 minutes. (SERVES 4 OR 5)

BAKED CRAB SALAD

★

1 cup crab meat

1 cup soft bread crumbs

1 cup whipping cream

1½ cups mayonnaise

6 cooked hard-boiled eggs, chopped

1 teaspoon minced parsley

1 teaspoon minced onion

½ teaspoon salt

½ cup quartered blanched almonds

½ cup buttered crumbs

Preheat oven to 350 degrees. ★ Combine first four ingredients. Combine remaining ingredients except buttered crumbs, add to the crab mixture, mix well and scoop into casserole dish. Top with buttered crumbs and bake half an hour. (SERVES ABOUT 8)

BAKED CRAB

★

¼ cup butter, plus some for topping crab mixture

4 tablespoons flour

2 cups milk

1 teaspoon salt

⅛ teaspoon pepper

1 pound crab meat

2 hard-boiled eggs, peeled and chopped

½ cup chopped pimientos

1 cup blanched and slivered almonds

1 cup dry buttered bread crumbs

Garlic salt

Preheat oven to 350 degrees. ★ Melt ¼ cup butter in a skillet and make paste by adding flour and a little milk. Add the rest of the milk and the salt and pepper and cook until thickened. Add crab meat, eggs, pimientos, and almonds. Blend in a blender and place in individual crab shells. Sprinkle with bread crumbs and dot with butter. Heat through until bread crumbs brown. May be prepared in advance and frozen. (SERVES 6 TO 8)

BOILED SHRIMP

★

Shrimp boiled in the shells taste better, and it's easier to remove the shells after boiling. If you have boiled shrimp too long, you'll find that the shell sticks to the shrimp and is hard to remove. Boil shrimp only 1 to 1½ minutes. Always salt the water generously (1 teaspoon to a quart of water). I like to add some Zatarain's Crab Boil or just add a beer for taste. Bring the water to a boil, put the shrimp in, and when water boils again, start timing. Drain immediately after boiling. The quicker shrimp are peeled and deveined the better. Shrimp can be kept in the refrigerator 1 or 2 days at the most.

DILLY SHRIMP

★

2 pounds raw shrimp

¼ cup butter

2 tablespoons lemon juice

2 teaspoons Season-All seasoning

½ teaspoon dry mustard

⅛ teaspoon cayenne pepper

1 teaspoon dill weed

⅛ teaspoon black pepper

Dash of ginger

Shell and devein shrimp. Melt butter in skillet; add lemon juice and seasonings. Sauté shrimp in seasoned butter 8 to 10 minutes, turning once. Serve with toothpicks. *(SERVES 6)*

SHRIMP CHEESE PIE

ONE OF JOE'S FAVORITES

★

1 (9-inch) pie shell, unbaked

1 (6-ounce) package natural Swiss cheese slices

1 pound shrimp, cleaned and cooked

2 eggs

2 teaspoons flour

1 cup light cream

½ teaspoon dried parsley

½ teaspoon onion salt

½ teaspoon salt

Paprika for dusting

Preheat oven to 400 degrees. ★ Place half of cheese slices in bottom of pie shell, top with shrimp, then remaining cheese. Blend together eggs, flour, cream, parsley, and salts. Pour over cheese. Dust with paprika. Bake 40 to 45 minutes. Let stand 5 minutes before cutting. *(MAKES 6 SERVINGS)*

SKINNY SHRIMP

★

½ cup hot water

2 packages chicken bouillon
or cubes

¼ teaspoon garlic powder

¼ teaspoon butter extract

2 pounds large shrimp

Preheat oven to 400 degrees. ★ Mix all ingredients together except shrimp. Set aside. Wash shrimp, pat dry. Don't peel shrimp; slice in half and place on a cookie sheet. Spoon the mixture over shrimp—about a tablespoon over each— and put in oven. Baste each shrimp occasionally. Cook until shrimp turns white inside, about 10 minutes. *(SERVES ABOUT 4 OR 5)*

SHRIMP HURRY CURRY

★

2 tablespoons butter or margarine

1½ pounds small raw Texas
shrimp, peeled and cleaned

1 can condensed cream of shrimp
soup

1 can condensed cream of
mushroom soup

¾ cup sour cream

1½ teaspoons curry powder

2 tablespoons chopped parsley

About 2 cups cooked rice (use your
judgment)

Sauté shrimp in margarine for 3 to 5 minutes over low heat, stirring frequently. Add soups and stir until thoroughly blended. Stir in sour cream, curry powder, and parsley. Continue stirring until mixture is piping hot, then serve immediately on fluffy rice. *(MAKES 4 TO 6 SERVINGS)*

BROILED TROUT OR SNAPPER

★

Fillets of trout or snapper (about 2
or 3 fillets per person)

Salt and pepper to taste

½ stick butter, melted

2 tablespoons butter, (or more,
depending on amount of fish)
sliced into small pieces

1 lemon

Wash fish thoroughly and dry on paper towels. Salt and pepper both sides of each fillet. Place on foil-covered cookie sheet. Place about 6½ inches under broiler. Top each fillet with a small slice of butter. Broil 15 to 30 minutes depending on thickness of meat. Baste every 5 minutes with melted butter. In the last ten minutes of cooking time, squeeze lemon juice over fish. It is done when meat is white and flaky all the way through. Do not overcook.

BAKED RED FISH

★

1 whole red fish

Salt and pepper to taste

1 (8-ounce) can tomato sauce

1 (14.5-ounce) can tomatoes

½ onion, chopped

2 sticks celery, chopped

1 garlic clove, chopped

Preheat oven to 350 degrees. ★ Wash, dry, and salt and pepper fish to taste. Place whole fish in foil in deep, long oven pan. Add 1 can tomato sauce and 1 can tomatoes. Chop onions, celery, and garlic and add to sauce. Close up foil and bake until vegetables are soft. Baste. Bake for about 1 hour. (SERVES ABOUT 5 OR 6, DEPENDING ON SIZE OF FISH)

STUFFED FLOUNDER

★

½ cup plus 3 tablespoons butter

¼ cup chopped onion

1 (3-ounce) can broiled chopped mushrooms, drained, liquid reserved

1 (7½-ounce) can crab meat, drained

½ cup coarse saltine cracker crumbs

2 tablespoons snipped parsley

½ teaspoon salt

Dash of pepper

2 pounds flounder fillets

3 tablespoons flour

¼ teaspoon salt

1 cup milk (or more if needed for the right consistency)

⅓ cup dry white wine

4 ounces shredded Swiss cheese

Paprika for sprinkling

In a skillet, cook onion in ½ cup of the butter until tender, but not brown. Stir mushrooms into skillet with flaked crab, cracker crumbs, parsley, salt, and pepper. Spread over flounder fillets. Roll fillets and place, seam side down, in a 12 x 7½ x 2-inch baking dish. ★ In a saucepan, melt remaining 3 tablespoons butter, and blend in flour and salt. Add enough milk to mushroom liquid to make 1 ½ cups. Add this, with the wine, to saucepan. Cook and stir until thickened and bubbly. Pour over fillets. Bake at 400 degrees for 25 minutes. Sprinkle with cheese and paprika. Return to oven. Bake 10 minutes longer, or until fish flakes easily with fork. (SERVES 8)

BATTERED SHRIMP

★

1 cup flour

1 egg

Salt and pepper to taste

Milk to make a batter (about ½ cup)

1 pound shrimp

Oil for frying shrimp

Mix flour, egg, and salt and pepper together in a bowl. Add enough milk to make nice batter. Add shrimp; take out and fry until golden brown. (SERVES 2 TO 3)

CREOLE-STYLE FLOUNDER

★

2 tablespoons butter or margarine

1 large green bell pepper, sliced into thin strips

1½ cups sliced green onions, with tops

1 (14½ to 16-ounce) can tomatoes, chopped (2 cups)

1 (8-ounce) can tomato sauce

1 teaspoon salt, plus to taste

¼ teaspoon pepper, plus to taste

½ teaspoon thyme

1 bay leaf

1½ pounds fillet of flounder or other white fish

3 cups hot, cooked rice

Sauté green pepper and onions with tops in butter or margarine until tender. Stir in tomatoes, tomato sauce, 1 teaspoon salt, ¼ teaspoon pepper, thyme, and bay leaf. Simmer gently for 20 minutes. Remove bay leaf. Arrange fish fillets in a lightly greased, shallow baking pan. Season with salt and pepper to taste. Spoon sauce over fillets. Bake at 375 degrees for 15 minutes or until fish flakes easily with a fork. Serve over bed of rice. (SERVES 6 TO 8)

SALMON CROQUETTES

★

1 (14-ounce) can salmon

⅛ onion, chopped, or ½ teaspoon onion powder

2 eggs, beaten

½ tube saltine crackers

½ inch corn oil in skillet

Put salmon into a bowl. Add onion, eggs, and crackers, crushing them up in your hands as you put them in the bowl. Mix this together really well and then make patties and put on a plate. The patties can be whatever size you desire. I like to roll them in cornmeal and Mother likes them plain. Fry until lightly brown. This is good with rice pudding and cooked cabbage or other vegetable. *This used to be our Friday meal a lot growing up when you couldn't eat meat on Fridays.* (SERVES ABOUT 4 OR 5)

FRIED FISH

★

Fillets of fish (about 2 or 3 fillets per person)

Cornmeal, cracker meal, breading mix, or flour for coating fish

Salt & pepper to taste

½ inch oil in skillet

Lemon slices for garnish

Cut fillets into individual serving portions. Wash thoroughly and dry on paper towels. Place cornmeal or other meal or flour in bottom of a paper sack or plastic bag. Add salt and pepper to taste and shake fish in bag until well breaded. Fry until fish turns crisp and golden brown. Serve hot with lemon slices.

FISH–N–CHIPS

★

Corn oil for frying

2 pounds fish fillets

2 cups sifted flour

3 teaspoons salt

2 teaspoons baking powder

2 eggs, lightly beaten

1 cup milk

2 tablespoons oil

Heat oil over medium heat. Cut fish into serving-size pieces. Sift flour, salt, and baking powder together and roll fish in the mixture. Combine eggs, milk, and oil. Add remaining flour mixture left from coating fish and stir until smooth. Dip fish pieces in the batter and fry one to three pieces at a time in the hot oil until golden brown. Drain on paper towels. Serve hot with french fries.

(SERVES 4 OR 5)

BUTTERMILK-FRIED FILLETS

★

2 pounds fresh fish fillets

1 cup buttermilk

1 cup biscuit mix

1 teaspoon salt

½ inch corn oil in skillet

12 lemon wedges

Cut fillets into serving-size portions and place in a single layer in a shallow dish. Pour buttermilk over fillets and let stand for 30 minutes, turning once. Combine biscuit mix and salt. Remove fillets from buttermilk and roll in biscuit mix. Fry in moderately hot fat for 4 to 5 minutes or until golden brown. Turn carefully and fry 4 or 5 minutes longer or until fish is golden brown all over and flakes easily when tested with a fork. Drain on paper towels. Serve with lemon wedges. *(SERVES 6)*

TARTAR SAUCE

★

2 large white onions

4 medium sweet pickles

Juice of 1 lemon

1 cup mayonnaise

2 tablespoons sugar

2 teaspoons salt

1 teaspoon black pepper

With an electric mixer, blend the onions and pickles. Add lemon juice, mayonnaise, sugar, salt, and pepper. Mix well. *(MAKES ABOUT 2 CUPS OR ENOUGH FOR 8 PEOPLE)*

FRIED OYSTERS

★

Fresh oysters (about 6 per person, depending on size)

Corn oil for frying

MEAL

1½ cups cornmeal or flour or mixture of both

Salt and pepper to taste

BATTER

¾ cup milk

2 eggs

¼ teaspoon salt

¼ teaspoon pepper

Mix batter ingredients together, then mix meal ingredients together. Dip oysters in batter, then in meal. Heat oil to very hot. Fry oysters.

L & A GUMBO

★

½ pound bacon

1 large onion, chopped

2 cups celery, chopped

2 green bell peppers, chopped

2 garlic cloves, chopped

3 to 4 (14½-ounce) cans peeled tomatoes, with liquid

2 (14½-ounce) cans okra

Water as needed

1 small (14-ounce) bottle catsup

Worcestershire sauce to taste

Salt, pepper, thyme, oregano, curry powder, allspice, and bay leaves, all to taste

1 large fryer chicken, boiled, deboned, and finely chopped

Shrimp or crab or other preferred seafood, as much as you like

In a large pot, brown bacon and set aside. Sauté onion, celery, bell peppers, and garlic buttons in bacon grease. Then add tomatoes, with liquid, and okra. Add water throughout as needed. Also add catsup and Worcestershire sauce. Add a little of the other spices at a time and taste to get it to the way you like it. Simmer about 2 hours and then add the chicken and seafood you prefer. Simmer another 30 minutes.

CASSEROLES & RICE DISHES

CHICKEN-RICE BAKE

★

1 can cream of chicken soup

1 can cream of mushroom soup

3 cups water

1½ cups uncooked rice

1 large fryer, cut into serving pieces

Salt and pepper to taste

Preheat oven to 375 degrees. ★ Spray a 13 x 9-inch casserole dish with Pam. Put uncooked rice in the casserole dish. Mix cream of mushroom soup with 1½ cups water and pour over rice. Salt and pepper chicken and place in casserole on top of rice. Mix cream of chicken soup with remaining 1½ cups water and pour over chicken. Bake, uncovered, for about 1½ hours or until chicken is tender. Check after about 1 hour. (SERVES 5 OR 6)

Suggestions: If you need a little more than 1 chicken, just add a few pieces of cut up chicken (like breasts) and another can of soup. You would probably need to go to a little larger size casserole dish for this. ★ If you would like a little more gravy for the rice, just pour another can of soup over the chicken. ★ If you feel you would like more rice in the finished dish, just add more rice. Use 2 cups water for every cup of rice you add.

Grandma Anna Polasek, 1930s.

BROCCOLI-RICE CASSEROLE

★

½ stick butter

½ cup chopped onion

½ cup chopped celery

2 (10-ounce) packages frozen chopped broccoli, cooked

2 cups cooked rice (1 cup raw rice)

1 can condensed cream of mushroom or cream of chicken soup

½ (4-ounce) jar Cheez-Whiz (some recipes call for a 14-ounce jar)

1 (5-ounce) can water chestnuts, drained and sliced

Preheat oven to 350 degrees. ★ Sauté onion and celery in butter until soft and golden. Combine with broccoli, rice, soup, Cheez-Whiz and water chestnuts in a greased 2-quart casserole dish. Bake 20 to 30 minutes at 350 degrees. May be made in advance and refrigerated until ready to cook. May be frozen. Allow 45 minutes to 1 hour baking time if casserole is chilled or frozen. (SERVES 8)

BASIC FRIED RICE

★

3 tablespoons oil

2 green onions, chopped

2 eggs, lightly beaten

3 cups boiled rice (see recipe page 51), room temperature

½ teaspoon salt

1 tablespoon soy sauce

Heat 3 tablespoons oil in a wok over high heat. Add green onions and eggs and stir for 10 to 20 seconds. Add rice and stir briskly for 2 minutes more. Season with salt and soy sauce, mix well, and serve. Can be prepared ahead of time and reheated. (SERVES 4)

Variation: Substitute 1 tablespoon brown sauce or 1 tablespoon dark soy sauce for 1 tablespoon soy sauce if you like a darker color.

BARBECUED PORK FRIED RICE

★

3 tablespoons oil

2 green onions, chopped

2 eggs, lightly beaten

3 cups boiled rice (see recipe
   page 51), room temperature

1 cup barbecued pork, diced

½ teaspoon salt

1 tablespoon soy sauce

Heat oil in a wok over high heat. Add green onions and eggs and stir for 10 to 20 seconds. Add rice and pork; stir briskly for 2 minutes. Season with salt and soy sauce; mix well and serve. *(SERVES 4 TO 6)*

BEEF FRIED RICE

★

1 cup water

½ cup frozen peas and carrots

1 teaspoon salt

3 tablespoons oil

½ pound lean ground beef

2 green onions, chopped

2 eggs, lightly beaten

3 cups boiled rice, (see recipe
   page 51), room temperature

1 tablespoon soy sauce

In a small saucepan, bring water to a boil. Add peas and carrots and ¼ teaspoon of the salt. Cook over medium heat for 1 minute and drain. Heat 1 tablespoon of the oil in a wok over high heat. Add ground beef and another ¼ teaspoon salt, and brown. Drain off excess fat and transfer beef to a bowl. Rinse and dry the wok; heat remaining 2 tablespoons oil over high heat. Add green onions and eggs, and stir for 10 to 20 seconds. Add rice and stir briskly for 1 to 2 minutes or until rice is heated through. Return beef, peas, and carrots to the wok. Add remaining ½ teaspoon salt and soy sauce. Mix well and serve. *(SERVES 4 TO 6)*

CHICKEN FRIED RICE

★

½ uncooked chicken breast, boned
    and skinned

1 teaspoon cornstarch

1 teaspoon dry sherry

1 teaspoon soy sauce

2 teaspoons water

¼ pound fresh mung bean sprouts

4 tablespoons oil

2 green onions, chopped

2 eggs, lightly beaten

3 cups boiled rice (see recipe
    page 51), room temperature

¾ teaspoon salt

1 tablespoon soy sauce

Dice chicken into ¼-inch pieces. Transfer the chicken to a mixing bowl. Add cornstarch, sherry, soy sauce, and water and toss to coat thoroughly. Let stand for 5 minutes or longer. ★ Snap off the root ends of bean sprouts. Rinse bean sprouts in a pot of cold water and drain. Pile trimmed bean sprouts on a chopping board; cut into ½-inch pieces. ★ Heat 1 tablespoon of the oil in a wok over high heat. Add bean sprouts and stir-fry for 1 minute or less. Transfer to a colander to drain. Wipe the wok with a paper towel; heat another tablespoon oil over high heat. Add chicken. Stir-fry until chicken turns white and firm. Transfer chicken to a plate. Rinse and dry the wok; heat remaining 2 tablespoons oil over high heat. Add green onions and eggs and stir for 10 to 20 seconds. Add rice and stir briskly for 2 minutes or until rice is heated. Return chicken and bean sprouts to the wok. Add salt and soy sauce. Mix well and serve. (*SERVES 4 TO 5 PEOPLE*)

GOULASH
★

1 pound ground beef or leftovers

½ cup chopped onion

1 clove garlic or ⅛ teaspoon garlic powder

1 teaspoon salt

3 cups noodles

2 cups tomato juice

1 (3-ounce) can mushrooms

1 green bell pepper, chopped

1½ tablespoons Worcestershire sauce

1½ teaspoons celery salt

½ cup water

1 can of beef broth

Brown ground beef in Dutch oven with onion, garlic, and salt. Add noodles and the rest of the ingredients and simmer 20 minutes or until noodles are done. (SERVES 6 TO 8)

LASAGNA
★

1 pound ground chuck

Salt and pepper to taste

2 (15½-ounce) jars spaghetti sauce

1 pound cottage cheese

1 (1-pound) package lasagna noodles, cooked, drained, and separated

1 pound mozzarella cheese, coarsely grated

1 cup Parmesan cheese, grated

Sauté meat until brown. Drain and season with salt and pepper. Stir in spaghetti sauce. Spray a 9 x 13-inch pan with Pam and spread a thin layer of sauce. Lay ⅓ of the noodles over the sauce. Top noodles with ⅓ of the cottage cheese, ⅓ of the mozzarella cheese, ⅓ of the meat sauce and ⅓ of the Parmesan cheese. Repeat layers two more times, ending with Parmesan cheese. Bake at 350 degrees for 45 minutes. Cool 10 minutes before cutting into squares. May be made in advance and stored in refrigerator or frozen and used later. Add time for defrosting or baking refrigerated food. (SERVES ABOUT 6)

Agnes Polasek's mother, Agnes Kucera in 1934. Also, brothers Simon and Sylvester, and sister Martha. Agnes Polasek holding her son Theo Louis.

FOSTER'S MEXICAN DISH

★

2 pounds ground beef

Onion powder to sprinkle on
   ground beef

1 can cream of mushroom soup

1 can cream of chicken soup

1 (10-ounce) can enchilada sauce

Plain Doritos (about half a
   medium-size bag)

2 cups shredded Cheddar cheese

Sprinkle hamburger with onion powder, brown, and drain. Put cans of soup and enchilada sauce in and mix. Place one half of mixture in a 9 x 13-inch baking dish. Crush up some Doritos and sprinkle over meat and then put ¾ of the cheese over this. Then add the rest of the meat mixture and sprinkle some more crushed up Doritos and top with the rest of the cheese. Bake at 350 degrees for 30 minutes or heat for 15 minutes in the microwave. *(SERVES 6 TO 8)*

BEEFY MACARONI-AND-CHEESE CASSEROLE

★

1 package Kraft White Cheddar
   macaroni

1 can cream-of-chicken soup

1 (10-ounce) can Rotel diced
   tomatoes

1½ pounds ground beef

2 tablespoons black pepper

1 tablespoon onion powder

8 ounces Velveeta cheese, sliced

Prepare macaroni and cheese per package directions; add cream of chicken soup and tomatoes and mix well. Pour into a 13 x 9 x 2-inch casserole dish and spread evenly. Brown the ground beef with seasonings. Layer the beef over macaroni and cheese mixture. Place slices of Velveeta across top of meat. Bake at 350 degrees for 30 to 45 minutes until cheese starts to melt. *(SERVES ABOUT 6)*

Variation: Substitute chicken or sausage for the beef for variety. If substituting with sausage, you may prefer to leave out the pepper and onion powder.

JAMBALAYA

★

1½ pounds sausage or cubed beef

2 teaspoons salt, plus some for
   sprinkling on meat

Pepper to taste

3 tablespoons bacon drippings, if
   beef is used

3 tablespoons flour

4½ cups water

2 medium onions, chopped

1 bunch green onions, chopped

2 tablespoons parsley, chopped

2 cloves garlic, minced

2 cups rice

¾ teaspoon ground red pepper

Salt and pepper cubed beef (you don't need salt and pepper with sausage).
Using a heavy black pot, brown meat in bacon drippings (or sausage by itself).
Remove from pot and set aside. Add flour to pot and brown to a dark roux.
Add 2 cups water. Add onions, parsley, and garlic. Cook until soft. Then add
remaining 2½ cups water and rice, 2 teaspoons salt, pepper to taste, and
browned meat. When it comes to a boil, lower heat to lowest point and cook
for about 1 hour, covered tightly. When rice is done, remove lid and let cook
for a few minutes until rice dries a little. (SERVES 6 TO 8)

TATER TOT CASSEROLE

★

2 pounds ground beef

1 (16-ounce) bag frozen greenbeans

1 (30-ounce or 2-pound) bag frozen
   tater tots

1 can cream of chicken soup

½ cup milk

1 large onion, chopped

Preheat oven to 350 degrees. ★ Crumble raw ground hamburger into 9 x 13-
inch roasting pan. Sprinkle onions and green beans over meat. Arrange tater
tots on top. Mix soup and milk and pour over entire mixture. Bake for one
hour. (Do not add salt.) (SERVES ABOUT 6)

CHILI CHICKEN

★

1 egg

½ cup milk

1 cup flour

2 teaspoons chili powder

½ teaspoon garlic salt

½ teaspoon salt

1 teaspoon cumin powder

1 teaspoon MSG (flavor enhancer)

1 (2½ to 3-pound) fryer, cut into
    serving pieces

1 cup salad oil

Beat egg and milk together. Combine flour and seasonings. Dip chicken in egg, then flour mixture. Heat oil in electric skillet. Add chicken; brown all pieces. Reduce heat and cook about 45 minutes or until tender. *(SERVES ABOUT 4 OR 5)*

CHILI

★

1½ pounds ground beef

2 onions, chopped

1 (28-ounce) can whole tomatoes
    (or tomato sauce)

1 (6-ounce) can tomato paste

1 cup water

1 beef bouillon cube

1 (16-ounce) can red kidney beans

2 tablespoons diced green bell
    peppers

2 cloves garlic, minced

2 teaspoons salt

2 teaspoons dried oregano

2 teaspoons chili powder

½ teaspoon crushed red peppers

1 bay leaf

Brown ground beef and onion. Stir in remaining ingredients and simmer 30 minutes on stove or for the day in a slow cooker. *(SERVES 5 OR 6)*

FAST AND SIMPLE CHILI

★

1½ pounds ground beef

Salt and pepper to taste

1 (15-ounce) can chili (with or without beans)

Chili powder to taste

Brown meat and add salt and pepper. Drain all grease off. Add can of chili, let cook for a minute, and then see if you would like more chili powder than is in canned chili. I usually put in about 1 tablespoon. (SERVES ABOUT 5)

BOILED RICE

★

1 cup enriched, long-grain white rice

1-¾ cups water (use 1½ cups water if making fried rice)

Measure rice into a 2 to 3-quart casserole. Rinse with cold water a couple of times. Drain well and add 1¾ cups water. Cover and bring to a boil over high heat. Reduce heat to medium low, cover halfway and cook for 5 minutes or until water is almost absorbed. Cover tightly, reduce heat to low, and cook for 10 minutes more. (Do not lift lid.) Turn heat off and let stand for 10 minutes without lifting the lid. It is important to let the steam continue cooking rice. (SERVES 3 TO 4).

RICE DISH

★

1 cup uncooked rice

½ cup water

1 stick butter

1 can onion soup

1 can beef broth

1 (2½-ounce) jar mushrooms

Preheat oven to 400 degrees. ★ Combine all ingredients and place in a baking dish. Bake, covered, at 400 degrees 45 minutes. (SERVES ABOUT 6)

CHICKEN WITH ZUCCHINI

★

1 broiler-fryer chicken, cut into
  serving pieces

⅛ teaspoon pepper

½ teaspoon paprika

1½ teaspoons salt

1 medium onion, sliced

1 (16-ounce) can tomatoes

½ teaspoon dried leaf oregano

1 pound zucchini, sliced

Sprinkle chicken with pepper, paprika, and 1 teaspoon of the salt. Place on broiler rack about 4 inches from heat; broil until browned on both sides, turning once (about 10 minutes). Place chicken in large skillet. Add onion, tomatoes, oregano, and remaining ½ teaspoon salt. Cover; simmer 20 minutes. Add zucchini; cover and cook 10 minutes longer, until chicken and zucchini are fork tender. *(MAKES 4 SERVINGS)*

HAMBURGER CASSEROLE

★

2 pounds ground beef

1 bunch chopped green onions

2 teaspoons salt

2 teaspoons pepper

1 teaspoon sugar

1 garlic clove, minced

2 (8-ounce) cans tomato sauce

1 (12-ounce) package wide
  noodles, cooked

2 cups sour cream

1 (8-ounce) package cream cheese

Grated Cheddar cheese

Brown hamburger meat and onions and add salt, pepper, sugar, garlic, and tomato sauce. Simmer. Place in casserole dish. Put cooked noodles in casserole dish on top of meat mixture. Mix sour cream and cream cheese together and spread on top. Sprinkle cheese on top. Bake at 350 degrees for 1 hour. *(SERVES 6 TO 8)*

VEGETABLES

★

Agnes & Theo Polasek during their courting years
in Hungerford, Texas, 1930s.

MASHED POTATOES

★

Peel potatoes (about 1 per person) while your water is heating in a large pot. Mother cubes her potatoes and I slice mine—whatever you find better. Boil potatoes in water until they are soft. Then drain and add ¼ stick butter, salt and pepper to taste, and add a little milk to mixture when you are beating potatoes. I use an electric hand mixer to beat potatoes but there are other ways like the old fashioned potato masher. You are ready to serve.

MOTHER'S SOUR CREAM POTATOES

★

Boil as above and drain and put in ½ cup sour cream and salt and pepper to taste. Put salt and pepper directly on sour cream and mix and then mix into potatoes.

GLAZED ORANGE-CARROTS

★

3 cups thinly sliced carrots

2 cups water

¼ teaspoon salt

3 tablespoons butter

3 tablespoons orange marmalade

2 tablespoons chopped pecans or walnuts

Combine carrots, water, and salt in slow cooker. Cover and cook on high 2 to 3 hours or until carrots are done. Drain well. Stir in remaining ingredients. Cover and cook on high 20 to 30 minutes. (MAKES ENOUGH FOR ABOUT 4)

Alternate Method: Cook carrots in water until tender. Then bake in casserole with the other ingredients for ½ hour at 350 degrees.

GREEN BEAN CASSEROLE

★

2 (14½-ounce) cans cut green
beans, drained

¾ cup milk

1 can condensed cream of
mushroom soup

⅛ teaspoon black pepper

1 (2.8-ounce) can french fried
onions

Preheat oven to 350 degrees. ★ Combine beans, milk, soup, pepper, and ½ can of french fried onions. Pour into a 1½-quart casserole. Bake, uncovered, for 30 minutes. Top with remaining french fried onions and bake 5 minutes more.
(MAKES 6 SERVINGS)

MARINATED CABBAGE

★

1 head cabbage, quartered or sliced
thinly

1 (4-ounce) pimiento pepper,
chopped

1 green bell pepper, chopped

1 small onion, chopped

⅓ cup vinegar

2 teaspoons salt

¼ teaspoon pepper

2 tablespoons sugar

½ cup honey

⅔ cup salad oil

2 teaspoons dry mustard

Combine first four ingredients in a bowl and set aside. Combine remaining ingredients in a pot and bring to a boil. Pour over top of vegetables. Don't stir. Let cool and refrigerate. Keeps well in refrigerator for 2 weeks or more.
(MAKES ENOUGH FOR ABOUT 6 PEOPLE)

EASY CABBAGE COOKING

★

1 head cabbage

2 tablespoons butter

Salt and pepper to taste

1 teaspoon lemon juice

Chopped dill or tarragon to taste

To know the true joys of cabbage, just quarter it or cut it thinly, toss into salted water and cook for only a few minutes until it is barely tender and still crisp. Drain it, drench with butter, salt and pepper it and give it a bit of lemon juice and a touch of tarragon or chopped dill and serve it forthwith for one of the finest vegetables dishes known to man. (*MAKES 6 TO 8 SERVINGS*)

> *You can put all of the above after you are finished in a white sauce if you like—see page 30.* ★ *Alternate method: I also like to shred cabbage as if I was making cole slaw, then fry out 5 or 6 pieces of bacon, cut into tiny pieces and toss the shredded cabbage in the fat, turning it quickly several times until it braises to a light delicate brown and wilts down with the bacon flavor all through it. I then add a finely chopped garlic clove and a little white wine, cover the pan and simmer about 10 minutes, seasoning the cabbage with salt and pepper just before I dish it up.*

OKRA GUMBO

★

10 cups sliced okra

2 medium onions, sliced

1 green bell pepper, chopped

3 cups tomato juice

1 (6-ounce) can tomato paste

6 cups whole tomatoes, chopped

Rotel tomatoes or jalapeños to taste
   or 1 small jar picante sauce

2 garlic cloves, minced

Put everything in a pot and simmer slowly for 20 minutes or until vegetables are soft. (*SERVES 12 OR 14 PEOPLE*)

BREADS

★

Theo & Agnes Polasek's wedding reception
at farm in Hungerford, Texas, 1932..

GOLDEN CORN BREAD

★

1 cup yellow cornmeal	½ teaspoon salt
1 cup flour	1 cup milk
¼ cup sugar	1 egg
4 teaspoons baking powder	¼ cup corn oil

Preheat oven to 425 degrees. ★ In a bowl, combine cornmeal, flour, sugar, baking powder, and salt. Add milk, egg, and corn oil. Beat until fairly smooth—about 1 minute. Bake in a greased 8-inch-square baking pan for 20 to 25 minutes. (SERVES ABOUT 5 PEOPLE)

> For muffins or corn sticks, pour corn bread batter into greased muffin cups or hot, well-greased corn stick pans. Bake in preheated hot oven (425 degrees) 15 to 20 minutes. Makes 1 dozen muffins or about 14 corn sticks.

MEXICAN CORN BREAD

★

2 cups Old Tyme Corn Bread Mix	1 clove garlic, minced
2 eggs	2 jalapeños
1 can cream style corn	¾ cup buttermilk
¼ cup bacon drippings	½ pound grated Cheddar cheese
1 medium onion, chopped	

Mix all ingredients together and bake at 425 degrees for 30 minutes. (SERVES 6 TO 8 PEOPLE)

HOMEMADE BREAD

★

2 cups warm water

2 packages dry yeast

1 teaspoon sugar

1 teaspoon salt

2 tablespoons shortening

About ½ (5-pound) bag all-purpose flour (Hill Country Fair or Gold Medal)

Put water, yeast, and sugar in a large warm bowl and let stand until it foams. Then put some flour (about 1 cup) and salt and shortening into yeast mixture. Let it rise about 1 inch high and then put in the rest of the flour and mix. Allow to double in size and then form into two loaves. Place each on a floured board, knead, and shape into loaves. Let rise and double in size again and then bake at 350 degrees about 30 minutes or until brown. (MAKES 2 LOAVES)

The wedding couple, Agnes and Theo Polasek, 1932.

TUPPERWARE BREAD

★

9 cups unsifted flour (can use 5
   cups white and 4 wheat), plus
   some for kneading

1½ cups scalded milk

1½ cups water

⅔ cup sugar

4 eggs, beaten

2 teaspoons salt

2 packages yeast

2 sticks margarine, melted

Put flour in a large tupperware bowl and make a well in the middle. In another bowl mix together milk, water, sugar, eggs, salt, and yeast. Put on seal, burp, and let stand until seal pops off. Then add margarine; mix and knead. Add flour if needed for kneading or right consistency. Put seal on and burp. Let stand until seal pops off. Divide into 3 parts and place on floured cloth. With a rolling pin, roll each part of dough separately into a 15 x 6-inch rectangle, then roll jelly-roll style. Roll ends under and put on greased cookie sheet. Let rise until doubled. Bake 30 minutes at 350 degrees. (MAKES 3 LOAVES)

KOLACHES

★

1 yeast cake, or 1 package dry yeast
   (handle yeast carefully when putting in water so you don't kill it)

1 cup warm water

1 tablespoon sugar

3¼ to 3¾ cup flour, plus some for
   working dough

½ stick margarine, melted, plus extra

1 cup warm evaporated milk

1 egg

Pinch of salt

½ cup sugar

Butter for spreading on top

Desired fruit or other filling, such
   as prunes, apricots, apples, cheese
   (page 62), or poppy seed (page 62)

Carefully put into a large warm bowl 1 yeast cake or dried yeast, warm (not hot) water, and sugar and carefully stir to dissolve yeast. Add ¾ cup flour. Let rise about 30 minutes, beating every 5 minutes. Add melted margarine, evaporated milk, egg, salt, and ½ cup sugar. Then add 2½ to 3 cups flour to make dough. Beat every 10 minutes (3 times). Let rise again. Then start taking a spoonful at a time out of bowl. Place spoonfuls onto floured board and roll them around in a little flour. ★ After you have enough of them to make a full pan, stop and roll each spoonful in your floured hands to make a ball and place on cookie sheet (like cookies). You must coat your hands with flour while working with this dough. If it is too sticky, roll the ball in the flour again. The more flour you use the tougher the kolach will be. When the pan is full, brush kolach tops with melted butter. Set aside and start on another pan until all the dough is gone. As the kolaches rise and are about double their original size, start putting in the fruit or whatever you desire. Put it in the center of each kolach, poking it down a little. With cheese or poppy seed filling, you can put it in the center as you would fruit, or flatten dough ball, fill, bring sides up, pinch closed, and turn over. Put a little bit of streusel topping on top. Let rise about double again and then bake at 325 degrees until light brown (about 30 minutes). *(MAKES ABOUT 60 KOLACHES)* ★ Fruit topping: I usually cook my fruit in water the night before and add sugar (according to taste). Barely cover fruit with water and cook until soft. Mash up for topping and sweeten to taste. ★ Streusel Topping: With a fork, mix together 1 cup sugar and 1 cup flour and enough melted butter (about ¼ cup) to make it kind of like oatmeal. You can also use this for Dewberry Pie (page 70). Freezes well. *(MAKES 10 PIES)*

You can also use this dough with sausage. Get small, cooked sausages. Flatten each kolach ball and roll up sausage by just bringing sides together; pinch closed and turn over. Bake same as kolaches.

CHEESE FILLING

★

1 cup small curd cottage cheese	¼ teaspoon salt
2 egg yolks	¼ teaspoon cinnamon
½ cup sugar	½ teaspoon vanilla

Drain cottage cheese until very dry. Then combine all ingredients and cream.
(MAKES ENOUGH FOR 1 KOLACH RECIPE)

POPPY SEED FILLING

★

1 pound poppy seeds	½ teaspoon cinnamon
2 cups milk	1½ cups sugar
½ stick butter	1 teaspoon to 1 tablespoon flour

Grind poppy seeds. Put all the ingredients except flour in a saucepan and bring
to a boil. Simmer 5 minutes. Add flour if needed to thicken.
(MAKES ENOUGH FOR 1 KOLACH RECIPE)

CELESTINE CRUST

★

3 eggs	¼ cup milk
3 tablespoons sugar, plus some for sprinkling	Dash of salt
	about 1¼ cups flour
1 tablespoon butter	Vegetable shortening for frying

Mix all ingredients together and blend well. Add enough flour to make a soft
dough (about like for noodles). Work dough out well and then roll out really
thin—the thinner the better. Cut in squares or diamond shapes. Prick with a
fork and fry in vegetable shortening till light brown. Take out and sprinkle
sugar on tops. (MAKES 2½ DOZEN)

DESSERTS

★

Agnes Marie with brothers Theo Louis, and Johnny Joe, 1938.

PIES

CRISCO PIE CRUST

★

2 cups sifted flour   ¾ cups Crisco shortening

1 teaspoon salt   ¼ cup water

Preheat oven to 400 degrees. ★ Place flour in a bowl along with salt and mix. Add Crisco and blend with pastry blender or fork. Add water and blend with fork and make into a ball. Place on floured cloth or floured waxed paper and roll out to fit pie pan. Place in a pie pan and prick crust bottom several times with a fork to avoid bubbles. Bake for 10 minutes or until lightly brown.

CORN OIL CRUST

★

1½ cups flour   ¾ teaspoon salt

½ cup oil   2 tablespoons milk

1 teaspoon sugar

Preheat oven to 400 degrees. ★ Mix ingredients in pie pan and spread out to fit pan. Bake for 10 minutes.

CHOCOLATE PIE

★

3 egg yolks

1 cup sugar

3 tablespoons flour

2 tablespoons cocoa

1-½ cups milk

1 teaspoon vanilla

2 tablespoons butter

1 baked pie crust (Corn Oil or
Crisco Pie Crust, opposite page)

MERINGUE

3 egg whites

2 tablespoons sugar

½ teaspoon vanilla

½ teaspoon cream of tartar

Mix first four ingredients together and then add milk, vanilla, and butter. Mix well. Cook over medium heat until thick and pour into crust. ★ Make meringue. Beat egg whites stiff (when bowl can be turned over without spilling) and add sugar, vanilla, and cream of tartar. ★ Place meringue on top of custard and place pie back in the oven at 350 degrees for about 15 minutes or until brown.

If you desire a taller meringue, use 5 egg whites and 4 tablespoons sugar.

Polasek home, Wharton, Texas, and The Little Inn
Hamburger stand where we served school children, 1949.

BANANA BREEZE PIE

★

NO-BAKE CRUST

⅓ cup butter

¼ cup sugar

½ teaspoon cinnamon

1 cup crushed Kellogg's Corn
   Flakes

NO-COOK FILLING

1 (8-ounce) package cream cheese,
   softened

1 can sweetened condensed milk

⅓ cup plus 2 tablespoons bottled
   lemon juice

1 teaspoon vanilla extract

5 medium-size ripe bananas

Melt butter, sugar, and cinnamon in a small saucepan over low heat, stirring constantly until bubbles form around edges of pan. Remove from heat. Add Corn flakes; mix well. Press mixture evenly into 9-inch pie pan. Chill. ★ Beat cream cheese until light and fluffy. Add sweetened condensed milk. Blend thoroughly. Add ⅓ cup of the lemon juice and vanilla and stir until thickened. Slice three of the bananas and line crust with slices. Turn filling into crust. Refrigerate 2 to 3 hours or until firm (do not freeze). Slice the other two bananas and dip in remaining lemon juice. Garnish top of pie with banana slices.

FRESH APPLE PIE

★

¾ cup sugar

1 tablespoon cornstarch

1 teaspoon ground cinnamon

6 cups peeled, cored, and sliced
   apples

1 tablespoon lemon juice

1 recipe double crust pastry (double
   Crisco Pie Crust, page 64)

1 tablespoon butter

Preheat oven at 425 degrees. ★ Stir together first 3 ingredients. Toss with apples and lemon juice until coated. Turn into pastry-lined 9-inch pie plate. Dot with butter. Cover with top crust. Seal and flute edge; make slits in top. Bake for 50 minutes or until crust is golden brown.

KENTUCKY BOURBON FUDGE PIE

★

6 ounces semi-sweet chocolate

6 ounces unsalted butter

6 eggs

1½ cups sugar

½ teaspoon vanilla

3 tablespoons Kentucky bourbon

¾ cup unbleached white flour

1 baked Pecan Pie Crust (recipe page 68)

Place the chocolate and butter in a small bowl. Place it in the oven at 250 degrees to melt or melt in microwave, about 45 seconds. Remove when it appears to be about ⅔ melted and turn oven heat up to 350 degrees. Stir the chocolate mixture with a wooden spoon until completely smooth. ★ Break the eggs into a large mixing bowl. Gradually add the sugar while vigorously beating with a whisk. Beat until the mixture lightens in color and thickens slightly. Continue whisking while gradually adding the melted chocolate and butter mixture to the egg mixture. When well combined, stir in the vanilla and bourbon. Sift the flour over the chocolate mixture and gently stir with a spoon until barely incorporated. If you overbeat at this point, the pie will become heavy and very dense in texture. Once the flour is added, stirring must be kept to a minimum. ★ Pour into pie crust. Place on a baking sheet in the center of oven. Bake for 30 to 35 minutes. The top will have a firm crust and the center will be soft. Remove from the oven and cool at least 2 hours before serving.

PECAN PIE
(MOTHER'S)

★

3 eggs, beaten

¾ cup sugar

2 tablespoons butter

¾ cup Karo syrup

⅛ teaspoon salt

1 cup pecans

1 unbaked pie shell

Preheat oven to 375 degrees. ★ Beat eggs, add other ingredients and mix; in unbaked pie shell. Bake until center is firm, about 30 to 40 minutes.

PECAN PIE CRUST

★

3 tablespoons sugar

1½ cups unbleached white flour

½ cup unsalted butter, cut into
   ½-inch pieces

1 egg, beaten

½ teaspoon vanilla

5 ounces ground or finely chopped
   pecans

Preheat oven to 350 degrees. ★ Combine sugar and flour. Work butter pieces into the combined dry ingredients using your fingertips. When the mixture resembles coarse oatmeal, drizzle beaten egg over it with a fork. Add the vanilla and pecans and continue working the mixture with your fingers until it comes together to form a dough. ★ Place the dough in a 9- or 10-inch round pan with a removable bottom. Using your fingertips, press the dough 1-½ inches up the sides. Press the remaining dough uniformly over the bottom of the pan. Line the crust with a sheet of aluminum foil, pressing gently against the sides. Fill the foil with 2 cups raw rice or beans. Place on the bottom shelf of the preheated oven for 15 minutes. Remove the foil and return to the oven for 10 to 15 minutes. Take out foil and rice.

MYSTERY PECAN PIE

★

1 (8-ounce) package cream cheese

⅓ cup plus ¼ cup sugar

4 eggs

2 teaspoons vanilla

¼ teaspoon salt

1¼ cups chopped pecans

1 cup corn syrup

Preheat oven to 375 degrees. ★ Beat cream cheese with ⅓ cup of the sugar, 1 egg, 1 teaspoon vanilla, and salt until thick and creamy. Spread in bottom of pie pan and sprinkle with pecans. Set aside. ★ Mix by hand 3 remaining eggs until blended; add remaining ¼ cup sugar, remaining teaspoon vanilla, and corn syrup. Pour over pecans. Bake for 40 to 45 minutes.

LEMON CHEESECAKE PIE

★

1½ cups undiluted evaporated milk

1 (3½-ounce) package instant lemon-flavored pudding and pie filling

2 (8-ounce) packages cream cheese, softened

1 (6-ounce) can frozen lemonade concentrate, thawed

1 graham cracker crust

1 cup (8 ounces) whipping cream, whipped

In small mixing bowl, combine evaporated milk and pudding mix; beat 2 minutes. Set aside. ★ In a large mixing bowl, beat cream cheese until light and fluffy. Gradually add lemonade concentrate; continue beating until smooth, light, and fluffy, 3 to 4 minutes. Fold pudding mixture into cream cheese mixture, blending thoroughly. Pour filling into crust. Chill 3 to 4 hours or overnight. Top with whipped cream.

PEACH PIE OR COBBLER

★

1 (29-ounce) can sliced peaches, drained, syrup reserved

½ cup sugar

2 tablespoons enriched flour

⅛ teaspoon salt

¼ cup butter

2 teaspoons lemon juice

1 recipe double crust pastry (double Crisco Pie Crust, page 64)

Place drained peaches in pastry-lined pie pan. Then, in a saucepan, combine sugar, flour, salt, ¼ cup of the peach syrup, and butter. Bring to a boil until it thickens a little and changes color a little. Add lemon juice. Pour over peaches and make lattice top crust or place second crust over peaches and make some holes in top. If making a cobbler use the same recipe but place bottom crust in baking dish and lattice top. You may want to double recipe for cobbler.

RAISIN PIE

★

1½ cups golden raisins

1½ cups dark raisins

½ cup sugar

½ cup flour

½ teaspoon salt

grated rind of lemon

2 tablespoons lemon juice

1 recipe double crust pastry (double Crisco Pie Crust, page 64)

Preheat oven to 425 degrees. ★ Mix all filling ingredients together and put in unbaked pie crust. Top with second crust. You can brush the top pie crust (before you put it in oven) with 1 tablespoon cream and 1 egg yolk (beaten) if you want a shiny top crust. Bake for 20 minutes. Cut heat down to 250 degrees and bake for 45 minutes more.

DEWBERRY PIE

(Mother's)

★

1 recipe Kolaches (page 60)

½ cup sugar

1 tablespoon cornstarch

Streusel topping (from kolach recipe, page 61)

Preheat oven to 325 to 350 degrees (depending on your oven). ★ Spread dough in pie pan and as it rises spread it out to sides of pan. Place dewberries all over crust. Mix sugar and cornstarch. Sprinkle over dewberries and put streusel on top of that. Bake until edges are brown and middle is firm.

TV PUMPKIN PIE

★

½ cup brown sugar

½ cup sugar

1 tablespoon flour

Pinch of salt

1 teaspoon ginger

1 teaspoon cinnamon

½ teaspoon ground nutmeg

½ teaspoon ground cloves

½ teaspoon allspice

1 cup milk

1 cup canned pumpkin or
   pumpkin meat scraped from
   inside a fresh pumpkin

2 egg whites, whipped

Preheat oven to 450 degrees. ★ Combine sugars, flour, salt, ginger, cinnamon, nutmeg, cloves, and allspice and mix well. Then add milk and pumpkin and mix well. Add egg whites and mix in. Bake 15 minutes at 450 degrees and then at 350 degrees for 45 minutes.

ICE CREAM PIE

★

½ gallon vanilla ice cream,
   softened

½ cup plus 1 tablespoon lemon juice
   (about 1 large or 2 small lemons)

1 cup sour cream

1 teaspoon vanilla

Grated rind of 1 lemon

1 graham cracker crust

1 cup frozen raspberries, thawed
   (or fruit of your choice)

Sugar to taste

Mix ice cream, ½ cup of the lemon juice, sour cream, vanilla, and lemon rind and place in pie crust (or you can serve in dessert glasses). Refreeze. ★ Mix fruit with about 1 tablespoon lemon juice and sugar to taste. Purée and spoon over pie slices or dessert cups.

SUMMERTIME LIME PIE

★

1 (9-ounce) can crushed pineapple, drained, syrup reserved

¼ cup lime juice

1 (3-ounce) box lime gelatin

1 (8-ounce) package cream cheese, softened

¾ cup sugar

1 teaspoon grated lime rind

5 to 6 drops green food coloring

1 cup evaporated milk

2 tablespoons lemon juice

1 (9-inch) graham cracker pie crust

Add enough water to pineapple syrup to make 1 cup. In a saucepan, combine pineapple syrup with water, and lime juice. Heat to boiling and remove from heat. Stir in gelatin until dissolved. In a 3-quart bowl, beat cream cheese, sugar, pineapple, lime rind, and food coloring with an electric mixer at medium speed until creamy. Add gelatin mixture gradually at low speed. Beat until well mixed. Chill until mixture is very thick, but not firm, about 10 minutes. Meanwhile, chill evaporated milk in ice tray until almost frozen at edges. Put ice-cold milk into cold 1½ quart bowl. Using cold beaters, whip at high speed until fluffy. Add lemon juice and whip until stiff. Add to chilled cream cheese mixture and mix at low speed. Chill 15 minutes, or until mixture is firm enough to mound. Heap into pie crust. Chill until firm, 2 or 3 hours.

ICEBOX CHERRY PIE

★

1 can sweetened condensed milk

1 can cherry pie filling mix

½ teaspoon vanilla

1 cup pecans

¼ cup lemon juice

1 baked pie shell (Crisco Pie Crust, page 64) or graham cracker crust

Combine all filling ingredients and pour into baked pie shell. Refrigerate at least a few hours or overnight.

LEMON MERINGUE PIE

★

1 cup plus 4 tablespoons sugar

3 tablespoons plus 1½ teaspoons
  cornstarch

Freshly grated peel of 1 lemon

¼ cup freshly squeezed lemon juice

3 eggs, separated

1 tablespoon butter

1½ cups boiling water

A few drops yellow food coloring

1 teaspoon vanilla

1 (8-inch) baked pie

1 pie crust (Crisco Pie Crust, page
  64)

Preheat oven to 350 degrees. ★ In a saucepan, thoroughly combine 1 cup plus 2 tablespoons of the sugar and cornstarch. Add lemon peel, lemon juice, and beaten egg yolks, blending until very smooth. Add butter and gradually stir in water. Bring to a boil over medium heat, stirring constantly. Boil 2 to 3 minutes. Stir in food coloring. Cool while preparing meringue. ★ Beat egg whites until stiff (when bowl can be turned upside down without spilling). Add remaining 2 tablespoons sugar and vanilla. Pour warm filling into baked pie shell; top with meringue, sealing well at edges. Bake for 15 minutes or until golden brown. Cool on wire rack away from drafts.

COOL WHIP LEMON PIE

★

1 (6-ounce) can frozen lemonade
  concentrate, slightly thawed

1 (12-ounce) can evaporated milk

1 (8-ounce) tub Cool Whip

1 graham cracker crust

Mix lemonade and milk together, then blend into Cool Whip and pour into pie crust. Refrigerate 4 hours and serve.

GRASSHOPPER PIE

★

14 chocolate Hydrox cookies,
   crushed

¼ cup margarine, melted

26 large marshmallows

½ cup milk

4 drops green food coloring

1 jigger (1½ ounces) white créme de
   menthe

1 jigger (1½ ounces) white créme de
   cacao

½ pint whipping cream, whipped

Combine cookies and margarine and press in a pie pan. ★ Melt marshmallows
in milk in a double boiler and cool. Add food coloring, créme de menthe, and
créme de cacao. Fold in whipping cream. Pour into pie shell. Chill at least 3 to
4 hours before serving.

Agnes Brandl Kucera holding Agnes Foster
along with her family, 1939. (Agnes Polasek on left).

COOKIES & BARS

OATMEAL CRISPS

★

2 cups shortening

2 cups brown sugar

2 cups sugar

4 eggs

2 teaspoons vanilla

3 cups sifted flour

2 teaspoons salt

2 teaspoons baking soda

6 cups quick-cooking rolled oats (uncooked)

Your favorite nuts (optional)

Preheat oven at 350 degrees. ★ Thoroughly cream together shortening and sugars. Add eggs and vanilla. Beat well. Sift together flour, salt, and baking soda and add to creamed mixture. Stir in oats (and nuts if desired). Mix by hand. ★ You can form dough in rolls (1 to 1½ inches in diameter and wrap in waxed paper), refrigerate overnight, and then slice cookies about ¼-inch thick with a sharp knife. Or what I do is drop by spoonfuls onto cookie sheet and bake right away. Either way, bake on ungreased cookie sheet in a 350-degree oven for 10 minutes or until lightly brown. (MAKES ABOUT 5 DOZEN)

OATMEAL COOKIES

★

½ cup evaporated milk

½ cup margarine

2 squares of chocolate

2 cups sugar

¼ teaspoon salt

2 cups oats

½ cup peanut butter

2 teaspoons vanilla

Put all ingredients in a pot at one time. Bring to a bubbling boil. Cook 1 minute and let cool. Drop by tablespoonfuls onto waxed paper. (MAKES 3 DOZEN)

FORGOTTEN COOKIES

★

2 egg whites	Pinch of salt
⅔ cup sugar	1 cup pecans, chopped
1 teaspoon vanilla	1 cup semi-sweet chocolate bits

Preheat oven to 350 degrees. ★ Beat egg whites until foamy. Gradually add sugar, vanilla, and salt. Beat very stiff. Fold in nuts and chocolate bits. Drop by spoonfuls onto foil-covered cookie sheet. Turn off oven and place cookies in oven. Leave them in until oven is cold. (MAKES 3½ DOZEN)

> Cookies may be tinted with food coloring just before adding nuts and chocolate bits.

DATE DROPS

★

½ cup shortening	1 teaspoon baking powder
¾ cup packed brown sugar	½ teaspoon salt
2 eggs	1 cup quick-cooking oats
¼ cup milk	1 cup chopped nuts
1½ cups sifted flour	1 cup chopped pitted dates

Preheat oven to 350 degrees. ★ Cream shortening and sugar. Add eggs and milk and combine well. Sift flour, baking powder, and salt together and add gradually. Add oats, nuts, and dates. Drop by teaspoonfuls onto a baking sheet. Bake 15 to 20 minutes. (MAKES 3 DOZEN FRUITCAKE-LIKE COOKIES)

ICEBOX COOKIES
★

1 cup shortening	3 cups flour
1½ cups brown sugar	1 teaspoon baking soda
1 cup sugar	1 teaspoon baking powder
2 eggs	1 cup chopped nuts

Cream shortening and sugars together. Add eggs. Sift together flour, baking soda, and baking powder and combine with creamed mixture. Add nuts. Form 2 rolls and wrap in waxed paper. Refrigerate overnight. ★ Preheat oven to 350 degrees. Slice cookies ¼-inch thick and bake on ungreased cookie sheet for about 10 to 12 minutes. (*MAKES 3 DOZEN*)

LADY FINGERS
★

½ cup egg whites (about 4 eggs)	1 teaspoon vanilla
¼ teaspoon cream of tartar	1¼ cups sifted cake flour
10 tablespoons sugar	½ teaspoon baking powder
2 egg yolks	Confectioners' sugar to sift on top
⅛ teaspoon salt	

Preheat oven at 450 degrees. ★ Beat egg whites to foam, add cream of tartar and gradually add 5 tablespoons of the sugar. Continue beating until mixture is very stiff. Then, in a separate bowl, beat egg yolks, adding salt and vanilla, until light and fluffy. Gradually add 5 remaining tablespoons of sugar and beat until thick. Fold egg yolk mixture into egg whites. Sift together flour and baking powder and fold in. Fill a cookie press using a number 32 tip. Form 3-inch fingers on a well-greased cookie sheet and bake for 6 to 8 minutes. Sift confectioners' sugar over the lady fingers as soon as you take them out of the oven. Remove from sheet immediately. (*MAKES 3 DOZEN*)

SUGAR COOKIES
★

1 cup butter	1 teaspoon baking powder
2 cups sugar	1 teaspoon nutmeg
3 eggs	½ teaspoon ground cloves
4 cups flour	

Preheat oven to 375 degrees. ★ Cream butter and sugar together. Beat in the eggs and then gradually add the dry ingredients while beating. Drop by teaspoonfuls onto an ungreased cookie sheet. Bake 6 to 10 minutes. (*MAKES 6 DOZEN*)

CHOCOLATE SUGAR COOKIES
★

½ cup shortening	1 tablespoon butter
1⅔ cup sugar	2 cups all-purpose flour
2 teaspoons vanilla	½ teaspoon salt
2 eggs	½ teaspoon baking powder
2 ounces unsweetened chocolate, or 7 tablespoons cocoa	1 teaspoon cinnamon (optional)
	½ cup chopped nuts (optional)

Preheat oven at 375 degrees. ★ Cream together shortening, sugar, and vanilla. Add eggs, unsweetened chocolate, and butter. Sift together flour, salt, baking powder, and cinnamon and add to mixture along with nuts. Drop 2 inches apart from ½ teaspoon onto greased baking sheets. Bake for 10 minutes or until golden brown. (*MAKES 50*)

MOLASSES SUGAR COOKIES

★

2¼ cups sifted flour

2 teaspoons baking soda

1 teaspoon cinnamon

½ teaspoon ground cloves

½ teaspoon ginger

½ teaspoon salt

¾ cup shortening

1 cup sugar, plus some for coating balls

¼ cup molasses

1 egg

Sift together flour, baking soda, cinnamon, cloves, ginger, and salt in a mixing bowl. Melt shortening in a saucepan over low heat; cool. To shortening add 1 cup sugar, molasses, and egg, beating after each. Add to dry ingredients; mix well. Refrigerate overnight in sealed mixing bowl. ★ Preheat oven to 375 degrees. ★ Shape dough into 1-inch balls using a rounded teaspoon of dough for each. Roll balls in sugar and arrange 2 inches apart on lightly greased baking sheet. Bake 8 to 10 minutes. Transfer hot cookies to wire rack to cool. (MAKES 5 TO 6 DOZEN COOKIES)

LEMON GINGER SNAPS

★

2 cups brown sugar

1 cup shortening

2 teaspoons lemon extract

2 eggs

4 cups flour

1 teaspoon ginger

1 teaspoon salt

2 teaspoons baking soda

2 teaspoons cream of tartar

Preheat oven to 350 degrees. ★ Cream sugar and shortening together. Add lemon extract and eggs. Sift dry ingredients together, combine with creamed mixture and mix well. Roll dough by heaping teaspoons in sugar and place on greased cookie sheet. Do not press down. Bake for 9 or 10 minutes. (MAKES 3½ TO 4 DOZEN)

WORLD'S BEST COOKIES
★

½ cup butter

½ cup sugar

½ cup brown sugar

1 egg

½ cup oil

½ cup oatmeal

½ cup crushed cornflakes

¼ cup Angel Flake sweetened coconut

½ cup of your favorite nuts

1¾ cups sifted flour

½ teaspoon salt

½ teaspoon baking soda

Preheat oven to 325 degrees. ★ Cream butter and sugars together; add egg and mix well. Add oil and mix well. Add oatmeal, cornflakes, coconut, and nuts. Mix well. Sift together flour, salt, and baking soda. Add to butter mixture and mix well. Drop by spoonfuls onto ungreased cookie sheet and bake for 12 to 15 minutes. (MAKES 4 DOZEN)

SNICKERDOODLES
★

1 cup soft shortening

1½ cups plus 2 tablespoons sugar

2 eggs

2¾ cups sifted flour

2 teaspoons cream of tartar

1 teaspoon baking soda

½ teaspoon salt

2 teaspoons cinnamon

Preheat oven to 400 degrees. ★ Blend together shortening, 1½ cups sugar, and eggs. Sift together flour, cream of tartar, baking soda, and salt. Add to creamed mixture. Combine cinnamon and remaining 2 tablespoons sugar. Form dough into balls the size of walnuts and roll in cinnamon-sugar mixture. Place balls two inches apart on ungreased cookie sheet. Bake for 8 to 10 minutes. Remove to rack to cool. (MAKES 2½ DOZEN)

TEXAS RANGER COOKIES

★

1 cup shortening

1 cup sugar

1 cup brown sugar

2 eggs

1 teaspoon vanilla

2 cups sifted flour

2 teaspoons baking soda

1 teaspoon baking powder

½ teaspoon salt

2 cups corn flakes

2 cups oats

1 cup Angel Flake sweetened coconut

1 cup pecans

1 cup raisins (optional)

Preheat oven to 375 degrees. ★ Put shortening and sugars in a bowl and blend. Add eggs and vanilla. Combine flour, baking soda, baking powder, and salt and add to mixture. Add corn flakes, oats, coconut, pecans, and raisins if desired. Drop onto ungreased cookie sheet and bake 8 to 10 minutes. (MAKES 5½ TO 6 DOZEN)

MARSHMALLOW TREATS

★

¾ cup sifted flour

1¼ cups sugar

¼ teaspoon salt

½ cup cocoa

⅓ cup Pet instant nonfat dry milk

½ cup soft shortening

1 egg

¼ cup water

1 teaspoon vanilla

½ cup your favorite nuts

Preheat oven to 350 degrees. ★ Combine all ingredients except nuts and blend well. Stir in nuts. Spread batter in greased 13 x 9-inch pan. Bake 30 minutes. (MAKES 25 SQUARES)

TOLL-HOUSE REFRIGERATOR COOKIES
★

1⅓ cups sifted flour

½ teaspoon salt

½ teaspoon baking soda

½ cup firmly packed brown sugar

½ cup sugar

½ cup soft butter

1 egg

½ teaspoon vanilla

1 (6-ounce) package Nestle's
  semi-sweet morsels (1 cup)

½ cup chopped Diamond walnuts

Sift together flour, salt, and baking soda; set aside. Combine sugars and butter in a bowl; beat until creamy. Beat in the egg and vanilla. Blend in the flour mixture. Stir in the chocolate morsels and walnuts. Shape into rolls, wrap in waxed paper, and chill for several hours or overnight. ★ Preheat oven to 375 degrees. ★ Unwrap chilled rolls and cut in 1-inch slices. Cut each slice into 4 sections. Place on ungreased cookie sheet. Bake 8 to 10 minutes. (MAKES 4 DOZEN)

DREAM COOKIES
★

1 cup sugar

2 sticks margarine

1 cup oil

2 eggs

2 teaspoons vanilla

4½ cups plain unsifted flour

1 teaspoon soda

1 teaspoon baking powder

1 teaspoon cream of tartar

Powdered sugar to coat cookies

Preheat oven to 325 degrees. ★ Combine first 5 ingredients and beat well. Sift together remaining ingredients, except powdered sugar, and add to creamed mixture. Mix well. Drop by scant teaspoonfuls onto ungreased cookie sheet. Bake for about 15 minutes or until light brown. While warm, roll in or sprinkle with powdered sugar. (MAKES 3½ DOZEN)

KISSING COOKIES
★

¾ cup butter

½ cup packed brown sugar

1 egg, separated

1½ cups flour

¼ teaspoon salt

Finely chopped pecans for coating dough balls

1 teaspoon vanilla

1 (13-ounce) package Hershey's Kisses

Preheat oven to 350 degrees. ★ Cream together butter and sugar. Stir in egg yolk (saving egg white) and add flour and salt. Let set for about 30 minutes to an hour in a cool place or put in refrigerator for 30 minutes. Then make dough into balls. ★ Beat egg white until very foamy. Roll the cookie balls in the egg white, then roll in pecans. Place on cookie sheet and make an indentation in each cookie with your finger. Bake for about 10 to 15 minutes. About 5 minutes before done, take cookies out and put a Hershey's Kiss in the indent. Return to oven for about 5 minutes more and then take cookies out.
(MAKES 2½ TO 3 DOZEN)

BROWNIES
★

¾ cup sifted flour

1¼ cups sugar

¼ teaspoon salt

½ cup cocoa

⅓ cup Pet instant nonfat dry milk

½ cup soft shortening

1 egg

¼ cup water

1 teaspoon vanilla

½ cup your favorite nuts

Preheat oven to 350 degrees. ★ Combine all ingredients except nuts and blend well. Stir in nuts. Spread batter in greased 13 x 9-inch pan. Bake 30 minutes.
(MAKES 25 SQUARES)

DANISH COOKIES

★

1¼ cups butter   3 cups flour

1¼ cups powdered sugar   ¼ teaspoon salt

1 egg   1 teaspoon vanilla

Preheat oven to 350 degrees. ★ Mix butter, sugar, and egg together. Add flour and salt, then vanilla. Use cookie press, and bake for 10 minutes. (MAKES 3 TO 3½ DOZEN)

FRUITCAKE COOKIES

★

¼ cup butter   ½ teaspoon cinnamon

½ cup brown sugar   ½ teaspoon nutmeg

¼ cup currant jelly   1 pound broken pecans

2 eggs   1 pound seedless raisins

2 teaspoons baking soda   ½ pound candied cherries, chopped

1½ tablespoons milk   ½ pound candied pineapple,
                                     chopped
1½ cups flour
                                  ½ pound citron, chopped
½ teaspoon allspice

½ teaspoon ground cloves

Preheat oven to 300 degrees. ★ Cream together butter, sugar, jelly, and eggs. Dissolve baking soda in milk and add to creamed mixture. Gradually add half the flour, sifted with the spices. Dredge nuts and fruits with remaining flour and stir into batter. Mix well. Drop spoonfuls onto buttered and floured cookie sheet and decorate with sliced candied cherries if desired. Bake for 20 minutes. These cookies ripen just as fruitcake does. (MAKES 2½ TO 3 DOZEN)

GINGERBREAD BOYS AND GIRLS

★

1 cup vegetable shortening	½ teaspoon salt
1 cup sugar	1 tablespoon ground ginger
1 egg	1 teaspoon cinnamon
1 cup light or dark molasses	1 teaspoon ground cloves
4 cups sifted enriched all-purpose flour	Decorating icing (Royal Icing, page 110, or Decorator's Icing, below)
2 teaspoons baking soda	

In large mixing bowl, cream shortening and sugar together until light and fluffy. Beat in egg and molasses. Add flour, baking soda, salt, and spices. Stir until a stiff dough is formed. Wrap dough in plastic wrap and refrigerate 3 hours. ★ Preheat oven to 375 degrees. ★ Cut dough into 4 pieces. On a floured surface, roll out dough to ¼-inch thickness. Cut gingerbread pattern from thin cardboard. Flour pattern and place on dough. Using the tip of a sharp knife, trace around patterns. Or, use cookie cutters. Place cookies on an ungreased cookie sheet about 1 inch apart. Bake 5 or 6 minutes or until puffed and brown around edges. Remove cookies to a wire rack; cool. *To use for hanging decorations on a tree, loop string under arms and tie securely on branch.* (MAKES ABOUT 12 GIRLS AND 12 BOYS)

DECORATOR'S ICING

★

⅓ cup egg whites	1 tablespoon rum extract
1 (1-pound) box confectioners' sugar	

In a medium bowl, beat egg whites and ½ the confectioners' sugar for 5 minutes with an electric mixer at high speed. Gradually beat in remaining sugar, ½ cup at a time until mixture is glossy and holds stiff peaks. Gradually beat in rum extract. ★ Using a pastry bag with a writing tip, outline each cookie. If desired, sprinkle with colored sugar, silver dragées, or other small decorative candies. After icing cookies, let stand at room temperature to harden.

CHEWY FUDGE SQUARES

★

1 box Duncan Hines butter recipe
   fudge cake mix

2 eggs

½ cup butter

1 cup miniature marshmallows

1 cup coarsely chopped walnuts

Preheat oven to 350 degrees. ★ Stir together cake mix, eggs, and butter until well blended (mixture will be stiff). Stir in marshmallows and walnuts. Spread mixture in pan. Bake for 25 to 30 minutes or until set in center. Cool, then cut into squares. (*MAKES 24 SQUARES*)

DATE LOAF SQUARES

★

1 cup dates

2 cups your favorite nuts

1 cup flour

2 teaspoons baking powder

1 egg, beaten

1 cup sugar

½ cup milk

1 teaspoon vanilla

Powdered sugar for coating squares
   (optional)

Preheat oven to 300 degrees. ★ Flour dates and nuts. Sift together remaining flour and baking powder and combine with nuts and dates. Combine egg, sugar, milk, and vanilla. Add to first mixture and bake in shallow pan lined with oiled wax paper, about 45 minutes. When done, cut into squares and roll in powdered sugar if desired. (*MAKES 24 SQUARES*)

CANDIED FRUIT SQUARES

★

1²⁄₃ cups chopped walnuts

½ cup sugar

½ cup packed light brown sugar

²⁄₃ cup corn syrup

⅓ cup water

2 (4-ounce) cans Angel Flake sweetened coconut

1 (4-ounce) jar diced mixed candied fruit

½ teaspoon salt

1 teaspoon vanilla

Grease a 9 x 9-inch pan. Sprinkle bottom with ²⁄₃ cup of the nuts. In a heavy, 2-quart saucepan, combine sugars, corn syrup, and water. Heat over medium flame, stirring to dissolve. Cook, not stirring, over medium flame to 248 degrees on candy thermometer, or to firm ball stage. Turn off flame. Stir in 2 ¾ cups of the coconut, fruit, salt, vanilla, and remaining 1 cup nuts. Spread in pan, top with the rest of the coconut. Chill, covered, overnight. Cut into squares. *(MAKES 49)*

DREAM BARS

★

¼ cup butter

1½ cups packed brown sugar

1 cup flour

2 eggs

1 teaspoon vanilla

1 cup corn flakes

1 cup coconut

1 cup pecans, chopped

Preheat oven to 350 degrees. ★ Mix butter, ½ cup brown sugar, and flour together. Press into a greased 9 x 13-inch pan and bake for 15 minutes. ★ Beat eggs with sugar until fluffy. Then mix in the rest of the ingredients and spread over baked layer. Bake 20 minutes and cut into squares while warm. *(MAKES 24 SQUARES)*

PUMPKIN CHEESECAKE BARS

★

2 cups unsifted flour

¾ cup firmly packed brown sugar

1½ cups chopped pecans
   or walnuts

½ cup butter, melted

3 eggs, beaten separately

2 teaspoons vanilla

1 (8-ounce) package cream cheese,
   softened

1 (14-ounce) can sweetened
   condensed milk

1 (16-ounce) can pumpkin (or
   about 2 cups scraped out of fresh
   pumpkin)

2 teaspoons pumpkin pie spice

Preheat oven to 350 degrees. ★ In medium bowl, combine flour, sugar, ½ cup of the nuts, and butter until crumbly. Stir in 1 egg and 1 teaspoon vanilla; mix well. Press into bottom of a 15 x 10-inch jellyroll pan. Bake 15 minutes. ★ Meanwhile, in large mixing bowl, beat cream cheese until fluffy. Beat in sweetened condensed milk, remaining eggs, pumpkin, pumpkin pie spice, and remaining vanilla until smooth. Pour over prepared crust; sprinkle remaining nuts on top. Bake 30 to 35 minutes or until set. Cool to room temperature; cut into bars. Store in refrigerator. (MAKES 48 BARS)

Tip: If you don't have pumpkin pic spicc, an approximate equivalent is:
1 teaspoon ground cinnamon,
½ teaspoon ground ginger, and
¼ teaspoon ground cloves.

Agnes Polasek Foster and brother Johnny Joe, 1939.

CAKES

GERMAN CHOCOLATE CAKE
★

1 cup butter	2½ cups flour
2 cups sugar	1 teaspoon baking soda
4 eggs, separated	½ teaspoon salt
1 square German sweet chocolate	1 cup buttermilk
½ cup water	1 teaspoon vanilla

Preheat oven to 350 degrees. ★ Cream together butter and sugar. Add egg yolks one at a time. Cream well. Melt chocolate in saucepan and add ½ cup water. Cook slowly until thick and creamy. Cool and add to butter and sugar. Cream. Sift flour, baking soda, and salt together and add alternately with buttermilk. Add vanilla. Beat egg whites and add to mixture, folding well. Bake in three greased 9-inch layer pans until cake tests done. Frost with German Chocolate Frosting 1 or 2 (page 107).

> To make this a pound cake: Leave out water, use only 2½ cups flour, and use whole egg at once. Cook in a bundt or angel food pan that has been well greased for about 1½ hours at 300 degrees. Place cake under tight-fitting cake cover while still hot, and leave covered until cold.

CAKE
★

1 cup butter	3 cups cake flour
2 cups sugar	½ teaspoon soda
4 whole eggs	½ teaspoon baking powder
1 cup buttermilk	1½ teaspoons vanilla

Preheat oven to 350 degrees. ★ Combine all ingredients, pour into three greased and floured 8- or 9-inch layer cake pans. Bake for 25 minutes.

YELLOW CHIFFON CAKE

★

2¼ cups cake flour

1½ cups sugar

3 tablespoons baking powder

1 teaspoon salt

½ cup corn oil

5 egg yolks

¾ cup cold water

2 teaspoons vanilla

2 teaspoons grated lemon rind

1 cup egg whites (7 or 8 eggs), beaten

½ teaspoon cream of tartar

Preheat oven to 325 degrees. ★ Mix flour, sugar, baking powder, and salt in a bowl. Make a well and add—in order—oil, egg yolks, water, vanilla, and lemon rind. Beat with spoon until smooth. In large mixing bowl, beat egg whites and cream of tartar until very stiff. Pour egg yolk mixture gradually over beaten egg whites, gently folding with rubber scraper just until blended. Pour into ungreased 10-inch tube pan, or 13 x 9½ x 2-inch oblong pan. Bake tube 55 minutes at 325 degrees, then 10 to 15 minutes at 350 degrees; oblong 45 to 50 minutes at 350 degrees or until cake tests done. Invert on funnel. Hang until cool.

PIÑA COLADA CAKE

★

1 (2-layer size) package extra moist white cake mix

¼ cup oil

3 eggs

1 cup (8 ounces) sour cream

1 (8½ ounce) can cream of coconut (I prefer Coco Lopez)

Preheat oven to 350 degrees. ★ In a large bowl, combine all ingredients and beat with an electric mixer. Pour into 2 greased and floured 9-inch layer cake pans. Bake for 30 minutes or until cake springs back when lightly touched. Cool in pan 15 minutes. Remove cake from pans and cool completely on rack. Frost with Piña Colada Frosting (page 110).

CHOCOLATE CAKE

★

1 stick margarine

½ cup Crisco shortening

1 cup water

¼ cup cocoa

2 cups sugar

2 cups flour

½ cup buttermilk

1 teaspoon baking soda

2 eggs, lightly beaten

FROSTING

1 stick margarine

⅓ cup milk

3½ teaspoons cocoa

1 (1-pound) box powdered sugar

1 cup Angel Flake sweetened
   coconut

Nuts (if desired)

Preheat oven to 350 degrees. ★ Combine margarine, shortening, water, and cocoa in a saucepan and bring to a boil. Sift together sugar and flour and add to the mixture. Combine buttermilk and baking soda and add to mixture, then add eggs. Bake as loaf cake at 350 degrees until middle springs back when touched (about 30 minutes). ★ Frosting: Combine all ingredients except nuts and bring to a boil. Add nuts. Frost immediately.

BUTTERMILK PLAIN CAKE

★

1 cup margarine

3 cups sugar

1 cup eggs (about 4 or 5)

1½ teaspoons vanilla

1 cup buttermilk

1 teaspoon baking soda

3 cups flour, sifted several times
   (measure after sifting)

Preheat oven to 350 degrees. ★ Cream together margarine, sugar, and eggs with electric mixer at high speed. Add vanilla. Combine buttermilk and baking soda. Add in flour gradually, alternating with buttermilk. Bake for about 1 hour or until it feels rather firm on top.

CHOCOLATE PUDDING CAKE

★

¾ cup plus ½ cup sugar

1 cup flour

¼ cup plus 2 tablespoons cocoa

2 teaspoons baking powder

¼ teaspoon salt

½ cup milk

3 tablespoons melted butter

1 teaspoon vanilla

½ cup firmly packed brown
      sugar

1½ cups boiling water

Preheat oven to 350 degrees. ★ Into 9-inch square pan, sift together ¾ cup sugar, flour, 2 tablespoons cocoa, baking powder, and salt. Stir in milk, melted butter, and vanilla and spread evenly in pan. Combine remaining ½ cup sugar, brown sugar and remaining ¼ cup cocoa. Pour over top of mixture in pan, then gently pour boiling water over this. Bake for 40 minutes. Serve with whipped cream or ice cream.

ITALIAN CREAM CAKE

★

1 teaspoon baking soda

1 cup buttermilk

1 cup sugar

½ cup butter

2 cups shortening

5 eggs, separated

2 cups sifted flour

1 teaspoon vanilla

1 cup chopped pecans

1 small can shredded coconut

Preheat oven to 325 degrees. ★ Combine baking soda and buttermilk in a 2-cup measuring cup and let stand a few minutes. Cream sugar, butter, and shortening together. Add egg yolks one at a time, beating well after each. Add buttermilk alternately with flour to creamed mixture. Stir in vanilla. Beat egg whites until stiff and fold in. Gently stir in pecans and coconut. Bake in three 9-inch greased and floured cake pans or a sheet pan. Bake 25 minutes or longer until cake is done. Frost with Cream Cheese Frosting (page 109).

SOUTHERN DEVIL'S FOOD CAKE

★

1 cup shortening

2½ cups sugar

2 eggs

1 teaspoon vanilla

1 teaspoon almond extract

2½ cups sifted cake flour

½ cup cocoa

2 teaspoons baking soda

Pinch of salt

1 cup buttermilk

1 cup boiling water

Preheat oven to 375 degrees. ★ Cream shortening and sugar thoroughly. Add eggs, vanilla, and almond extract and blend. Sift flour, then measure and sift three times with cocoa, baking soda, and salt. Add this to first mixture, alternating with the buttermilk. Then add the boiling water, stirring well. Bake in three greased 8-inch layer pans or a well-greased 9 x 12-inch loaf pan. Bake for 35 minutes or until center springs back up when lightly touched.

SOUR MILK DEVIL'S FOOD CAKE

★

1 cup sugar

½ cup vegetable shortening

2 eggs, well beaten

1½ cups flour

1 teaspoon baking soda

1 teaspoon baking powder

½ teaspoon salt

½ cup sour milk

2 squares baking chocolate

½ cup boiling water

1 teaspoon vanilla

Preheat oven to 375 degrees. ★ Cream sugar and shortening well. Add eggs. Sift together flour, baking soda, baking powder, and salt. Add to creamed mixture alternately with sour milk. Melt chocolate in boiling water and add to mixture. Add vanilla. Pour into 2 greased, floured 8- or 9-inch layer pans and bake about 30 minutes or until cake tests done. Frost with your favorite frosting such as Chocolate Fudge. ★ (To make sour milk if you forgot to get it, place 1½ teaspoons vinegar or lemon juice in ½ cup milk. Let sit 5 minutes.)

COKE CAKE
★

2 cups flour

2 cups sugar

1½ cups chopped marshmallows

½ cup shortening

½ cup butter

3 tablespoons cocoa

1 cup Coca Cola

½ cup buttermilk

1 teaspoon baking soda

2 eggs, beaten

ICING

⅓ cup margarine

3 tablespoons cocoa

6 tablespoons Coca Cola

1 (1-pound) box powdered sugar

1 cup chopped pecans

Preheat oven to 350 degrees. ★ Sift together flour and sugar; stir in marshmallows and set aside. In a saucepan, combine shortening, butter, cocoa, and Coke and bring to a boil. Remove from fire and pour over dry mixture. Stir (do not beat) in buttermilk, baking soda, and eggs. Pour into a greased tube pan and bake for 45 minutes or until done. ★ Icing: Combine first three ingredients and bring to a boil. When smooth, remove from fire, add sugar and pecans and ice cake.

7-UP POUND CAKE
★

2 sticks butter

½ cup shortening

2 cups sugar

5 eggs

3 cups flour

½ can (6-ounces) 7-Up

1 teaspoon vanilla

1 teaspoon butter extract

Preheat oven to 325 degrees. ★ Ingredients should be at room temperature. Cream butter and shortening with sugar. Add eggs, one at a time, beating well after each. Add flour alternately with 7-Up, vanilla, and butter extract. Bake in a large, greased tube pan until cake tests done, at least 1 hour.

PERFECT SPICE CAKE

★

2¼ cups sifted cake flour

1 teaspoon baking powder

1 teaspoon salt

1 teaspoon cinnamon

¾ teaspoon baking soda

¼ teaspoon ground cloves

1/16 teaspoon pepper

¾ cup butter

1 cup sugar

¾ cup brown sugar, firmly packed

1 teaspoon vanilla

3 eggs

1 cup buttermilk

1 recipe Cream Cheese Whipped
Frosting (page 96)

ORANGE DATE-NUT
FILLING

1 (8-ounce) package chopped dates
(1½ cups)

½ cup orange juice

1 teaspoon grated orange peel

¼ cup walnuts, chopped

Preheat oven to 350 degrees. ★ Sift together dry ingredients. Cream butter and sugars together until light and fluffy. Add vanilla. Add eggs, one at a time, beating after each addition. Add dry ingredients to butter mixture alternately with buttermilk, beating well. Pour into two 9-inch greased and floured cake pans. Bake 30 minutes or until done. Cool. Spread Orange Date-Nut Filling between layers and frost with Cream Cheese Whipped Frosting. ★ Orange Date-Nut Filling: In a saucepan, combine chopped dates with orange juice. Cook at medium heat and stir until dates are tender and mixture is thick, about 2 or 3 minutes. Add orange peel. Cool. Add walnuts.

CREAM CHEESE WHIPPED FROSTING

★

2 egg whites

¾ cup firmly packed brown sugar

¾ cup sugar

1½ teaspoons light corn syrup or
    ¼ teaspoon cream of tartar

⅓ cup cold water minus 2
    tablespoons

Dash of salt

1 teaspoon vanilla

1 (3-ounce) package cream cheese

Place all ingredients except vanilla and cream cheese in top of double boiler (not over heat). Beat 1 minute. Place over boiling water and beat constantly for 7 minutes. Remove from heat and add vanilla; cool to lukewarm. Transfer beaters from frosting to a separate bowl and add cream cheese; beat until smooth, then gently fold cream cheese mixture into the frosting. Do not beat.

PINK PARTY CAKE

★

2¼ cups sifted cake flour

4 teaspoons baking powder

1 teaspoon salt

1½ cups sugar

½ cup shortening

1 cup skim milk

1 teaspoon vanilla

½ to ⅔ cup egg whites (4 large)

10 drops red food coloring

Preheat oven to 350 degrees. ★ Sift together cake flour, baking powder, salt, and sugar. Add shortening, ⅔ cup of the skim milk, and vanilla. Beat with electric mixer at slow to medium speed for 2 minutes, scraping bowl frequently. Add remaining ⅓ cup milk and unbeaten egg whites. Beat 2 minutes longer, scraping bowl frequently. Tint batter with about 10 drops red food coloring during this last mixing period. Bake in two greased and floured 8-inch round cake pans for 30 to 35 minutes. When cool, frost with a fluffy boiled frosting—see frosting section.

STRAWBERRY CAKE

★

1 box white cake mix

3 tablespoons flour

1 (3-ounce) box strawberry Jell-O

1 cup corn oil

4 eggs

½ cup water

½ (10-ounce) package frozen strawberries, thawed, with juice

FROSTING

1 stick butter, melted

1 (1-pound) box powdered sugar,
sifted

½ (10-ounce) package frozen strawberries, thawed

Preheat oven to 300 degrees. ★ Mix together cake mix, flour, and Jell-O. Then, in a separate bowl, beat corn oil, eggs, and water and then add thawed strawberries. Combine with dry mixture; do not mix longer than necessary. Bake in greased, floured 9 x 13-inch pan for 50 minutes. ★ Frosting: Mix all ingredients together and frost.

GOLDEN BUTTER CAKE

★

⅔ cup soft butter

1¾ cups sugar

2 eggs

1½ teaspoons vanilla

3 cups sifted flour

2½ teaspoons baking powder

1 teaspoon salt

1¼ cups milk

Preheat oven to 350 degrees. ★ Combine first 4 ingredients and beat 5 minutes until fluffy. Combine dry ingredients and add to sugar-butter mixture alternately with milk, beginning and ending with dry ingredients. Pour into two ungreased 8- or 9-inch layer pans and bake 30 minutes.

LEMON CAKE

★

¼ cup butter

½ cup shortening

2 cups sugar

3 eggs

3 cups flour

½ teaspoon salt

½ teaspoon baking soda

1 cup buttermilk

1 teaspoon vanilla

1 teaspoon lemon juice

1 teaspoon grated lemon rind

FROSTING

½ stick butter

1 cup powdered sugar

Juice of 1 lemon

Preheat oven to 350 degrees. ★ Cream together butter, shortening, and sugar. Add eggs one at a time. Sift flour, salt, and baking soda together and fold into creamed mixture. Add buttermilk, vanilla, lemon juice, and rind. Mix well. Pour batter into a greased and floured tube pan. Bake for 1 hour. ★ Frosting: Melt butter. Add powdered sugar and lemon juice and mix. Pour over cake while it is still hot.

LEMON POUND CAKE

★

4 eggs

1⅓ cups evaporated milk

⅔ cup prepared lemon pudding

1 box yellow cake mix

1 teaspoon lemon extract

Preheat oven to 350 degrees. ★ Mix all ingredients and pour into ungreased angel food cake pan. Bake for 1 hour.

Ed Polasek and brother Theo with daughters Agnes and Alice.
Fishing trip to Oyster Lake, Texas, 1944.

OATMEAL CAKE

★

1¼ cups boiling water

1 cup oatmeal

½ cup Crisco shortening

1 cup sugar

1 cup brown sugar

2 eggs

1⅓ cups flour

½ teaspoon salt

1 teaspoon baking soda

1 teaspoon cinnamon

1 teaspoon vanilla

½ cup pecans

FROSTING

6 tablespoons butter

¼ cup table cream

1 teaspoon vanilla

1 cup fresh Angel Flake sweetened coconut

1 cup pecans

½ cup firmly packed brown sugar

Preheat oven to 350 degrees. ★ Pour boiling water over oatmeal. Let stand 20 minutes. Combine shortening, sugars, and eggs and beat well. Add to oatmeal and stir together. In a separate bowl combine flour, salt, baking soda, and cinnamon and add to oatmeal mixture. Add vanilla and nuts. Place in greased and floured 7 x 11-inch pan. Bake for 35 minutes. ★ Frosting: Mix all ingredients together and spread on cake while still warm. Put under broiler to get a little brown.

CHOPPED-APPLE CAKE

★

3 eggs

2 cups sugar

2 teaspoons vanilla

1 cup cooking oil

3 cups flour

½ teaspoon salt

1 teaspoon baking soda

2 teaspoons cinnamon

1 cup pecans, chopped

3 cups pared and chopped tart, juicy apples

Preheat oven to 350 degrees. ★ Beat eggs. Add sugar, vanilla, and oil. Beat well. Add flour, salt, baking soda, and cinnamon and beat. Batter should be very thick. Add chopped pecans and apples. Beat. Pour into greased, floured tube pan. Bake for 1 hour. ★ Note that there is no milk or other liquid. If you find you've chopped too many apples or nuts, put them in but add an extra egg.

PUMPKIN CAKE

★

4 eggs

2 cups sugar

1 cup corn oil

2 cups flour

2 teaspoons baking soda

2 teaspoons cinnamon

½ teaspoon salt

2 cups canned pumpkin or scraped from inside a fresh pumpkin

1 recipe Cream Cheese Frosting (page 109)

Preheat oven to 350 degrees. ★ Blend together eggs and sugar and add oil. Beat in dry ingredients and then add pumpkin. Pour in well-greased, floured 13 x 9-inch cake pan. Bake 55 minutes. Let stand in pan 10 minutes. Turn out on rack to cool. Frost with Cream Cheese Frosting (page 109) when cool.

BOILED CAKE
★

4 eggs, beaten	1 stick butter
2 cups sugar	1 cup milk
2 cups flour	1 1/2 teaspoons vanilla
2 teaspoons baking powder	

Preheat oven to 350 degrees. ★ Add sugar to beaten eggs and beat well.
Combine flour with baking powder and add to eggs. In a small saucepan, bring
butter and milk to a boil. Pour over the flour mixture and beat. Blend in vanilla.
The batter will be thin. Pour into greased 9 x 13-inch cake pan or baking dish
lined with waxed paper. Bake for about 50 minutes or until top is golden brown.

BANANA BREAD
★

1 stick butter, room temperature	1/2 teaspoon salt
3/4 cup sugar	1 cup whole wheat flour
2 eggs	3 large ripe bananas, mashed
1 cup flour	1 teaspoon vanilla
1 teaspoon baking soda	1/2 cup walnuts, chopped

Preheat oven to 350 degrees. ★ Cream butter and sugar together until light
and fluffy. Add eggs one at a time, beating well after each. Sift flour, baking
soda, and salt together and add to creamed mixture; mix. Stir in whole wheat
flour and add to mixture, mixing well. Fold in bananas, vanilla, and walnuts.
Pour mixture into greased 9 x 5 x 3-inch loaf pan. Bake 50 to 60 minutes or
until cake tester comes out clean. Cool in pan 10 minutes, then remove from
pan and place on rack. (MAKES 1 LOAF)

CARAMEL APPLE CAKE

★

1¾ cups flour (lightly spooned into measuring cup and leveled off)

1½ cups firmly packed brown sugar

1½ teaspoons cinnamon

½ teaspoon salt

½ teaspoon baking powder

½ teaspoon baking soda

1 teaspoon vanilla

¾ cup butter, softened

3 eggs

1½ cups peeled, finely chopped apples

1 cup chopped nuts

½ cup raisins

FROSTING

1½ cups powdered sugar

¼ teaspoon cinnamon

¼ cup butter, melted

½ teaspoon vanilla

3 to 4 teaspoons milk

Preheat oven to 350 degrees (325 for glass container). ★ In a large bowl, combine flour, sugar, cinnamon, salt, baking powder, baking soda, vanilla, butter and eggs. Beat 3 minutes at medium speed. Stir in apples, nuts, and raisins. Pour into greased 13 x 9-inch pan. Bake 30 to 40 minutes or until toothpick inserted in center comes out clean. Frost when cool. ★ Frosting: Blend all ingredients.

JELLY ROLL

★

4 eggs

1 cup sugar

Dash of salt

4 tablespoons hot milk

2 teaspoons vanilla

1 cup flour

2 teaspoons baking powder

About 1 cup of your favorite jelly,
or whipped cream or apple butter
for spreading on jelly roll

Powdered sugar for sprinkling on
jelly roll

Preheat oven to 350 degrees. ★ Beat together eggs, sugar, and salt and add hot milk and vanilla. Combine flour and baking powder and add to mixture. Pour into well-buttered pan or cookie sheet with sides and bake about 20 minutes. Turn onto damp cloth. Spread with jelly, whipped cream, or apple butter and roll. Wrap towel around roll until ready to serve; sprinkle with powdered sugar.

COFFEE CAKE

★

24 frozen Parker House rolls

1 cup sugar

1 teaspoon cinnamon

1 stick butter, cut into small pieces

1 (3-ounce) box butterscotch
pudding (not instant)

½ cup pecans

½ cup raisins

½ cup brown sugar

Grease bundt pan; put in frozen rolls. Sprinkle with sugar and cinnamon. Dot on ½ cup of the butter. Sprinkle butterscotch pudding mix, pecans, raisins, brown sugar, and remaining ½ stick butter on top. Put in oven overnight. Next morning, bake 30 minutes. Serve warm.

Grandma Agnes Kucera, October, 1938.

ORANGE-CARROT CAKE

★

3 cups sifted flour

2 teaspoons baking powder

1 teaspoon baking soda

½ teaspoon salt

2 teaspoons cinnamon

2 cups sugar

1½ cups corn oil

3 eggs

1 teaspoon vanilla

1 (8-ounce) can crushed
   pineapple, well drained

1 cup chopped pecans

2 cups finely grated carrots

FROSTING

1 (6-ounce) can frozen orange juice
   concentrate

1 cup sugar

Preheat oven to 350 degrees. ★ Sift together flour, baking powder, baking soda, salt, and cinnamon. Blend sugar and corn oil thoroughly with an electric mixer. Add eggs one at a time, beating well after each. Add vanilla. Turn mixer to lowest speed and blend in sifted dry ingredients. In separate bowl, combine pineapple, pecans, and grated carrots. Fold gently into batter. Pour batter into greased and floured 10-inch tube pan. Bake 1 to 1¼ hours. Frost while hot. ★ Combine ingredients in a saucepan and bring to a boil. Pour over hot cake in pan. Let stand 4 to 5 hours before serving.

FRUITCAKE

★

1 (1-pound) jar mixed candied fruit

1 cup each light and dark raisins

1 cup coarsely chopped pecans

½ cup sliced almonds

1½ cups sifted flour

½ sugar

½ cup firmly packed brown sugar

¼ cup softened margarine or butter

3 eggs

¼ cup peach brandy

¼ cup apple sauce

½ teaspoon almond extract

¼ teaspoon allspice

¼ teaspoon cinnamon

¼ teaspoon baking soda

Brandy-soaked cheesecloth

Preheat oven to 275 degrees. ★ In a plastic bag, combine candied fruit, raisins, nuts, and ½ cup of the flour. Toss to mix well. In a large bowl combine sugars and margarine or butter. Beat well until light and fluffy. Add eggs and continue beating 2 minutes longer. Stir in brandy, apple sauce, and almond extract. Combine remaining 1 cup flour, allspice, cinnamon, and baking soda and gradually add to mixture. Beat only until mixture is well dampened. Turn fruit and nut mixture into batter. Mix well with a large spoon. Spoon batter into greased and floured loaf pans and bake until cake is deep brown and a cake tester comes out clean when inserted into center, about 2½ hours for loaf size. ★ When cake is completely cool, wrap in brandy-soaked cheesecloth and then in foil; seal tightly. A metal cracker can is the perfect size to store it. Cake should be made by mid-October and left to age. Take out and re-soak cheesecloth with brandy every three weeks.

APPLESAUCE FRUITCAKE

★

1½ cups sweetened applesauce

½ cup vegetable shortening

1 cup sugar

1 (8-ounce) package dried, pitted dates, sliced (about 1½ cups)

1 (4-ounce) jar red glacé cherries, chopped (½ cup)

1 (8-ounce) can walnuts, chopped (2 cups)

2 cups seedless raisins

2¼ cups sifted flour

2 teaspoons baking soda

½ teaspoon salt

1 teaspoon cinnamon

½ teaspoon nutmeg

¼ teaspoon allspice

Preheat oven to 275 degrees. Grease two 8 x 4-inch loaf pans or one 9-inch tube pan. Line with foil and grease again. Set aside. ★ Combine applesauce, shortening, and sugar in a saucepan. Bring to a boil, then cook 5 minutes, stirring occasionally. Cool .★ Mix fruits, nuts, and raisins in a large bowl. Sift together flour, baking soda, salt, and spices. Gradually stir into fruit mixture. Stir in the cooled applesauce mixture. Pour batter into prepared loaf pans or the tube pan. Bake 1 hour and 40 minutes for loaf cakes or 2 hours for tube cake or until cakes test done. Cool cakes in pan on rack for about 30 minutes, then remove and cool completely before slicing. Wrap and store in tightly covered container.

Logene Foster's family, 1949. Sister Sybil Ray, mother Madeline, and father Leslie.

GERMAN CHOCOLATE FROSTING 1

★

1 cup sugar

3 egg yolks

¼ pound butter

½ cup evaporated milk

1 cup your favorite nuts, chopped

1 cup Angel Flake sweetened coconut

1 teaspoon vanilla

In a saucepan, cook sugar, egg yolks, butter, and evaporated milk over medium heat until thickened. Take off heat and add nuts, coconut, and vanilla.

GERMAN CHOCOLATE FROSTING 2

★

1 cup sugar

½ cup evaporated milk

1 stick margarine

1 teaspoon vanilla

1 cup coconut

½ cup pecans

Combine all ingredients and boil 2 minutes. This is harder to get thick than German Chocolate Frosting 1.

FLUFFY WHITE FROSTING

★

3 egg whites

¾ cup sugar

3 teaspoons light Karo syrup

¼ teaspoon cream of tartar

Combine all ingredients and beat while cooking in double boiler 4 minutes.

LEMON FROSTING

★

2¾ cups confectioners' sugar

½ teaspoon salt

1 egg

1 tablespoon light corn syrup

½ cup shortening

1 teaspoon vanilla

2 tablespoons lemon juice

1 tablespoon grated lemon peel

Mix confectioners' sugar, salt, and egg. Blend in syrup. Add shortening, vanilla, lemon juice, and lemon peel, mixing until smooth and creamy. Add more sugar to thicken or water to thin frosting, if required, until of spreading consistency. Frosts two 8- or 9-inch layers or a 13 x 9-inch cake.

LEMON BUTTER ICING

(WITH FRESH BANANA SLICES)

★

2 cups sugar

1 (5-ounce) can evaporated milk

Dash of salt

1 teaspoon vanilla

1 tablespoon butter

Juice of 1 lemon

5 fresh bananas

Put sugar and evaporated milk in small but heavy cooking pot. Rinse can with 1 tablespoon water and pour in. Add dash of salt and stir well. Cook, covered, for a few minutes, then remove lid. Let cook slowly until a drop of mixture forms a soft mound when dropped on saucer with water in it. Stir and watch closely. Remove from heat and add vanilla, butter, and lemon juice. Slice bananas on cake layer and completely cover with icing and then add second layer and repeat. Very good while warm.

WHITE ICING

★

1⅓ cups plus 3⅓ tablespoons sugar

⅓ cup water

2 tablespoons white corn syrup

2 egg whites, stiffly beaten

2 tablespoons powdered sugar

Mix sugar, water, and corn syrup. Cook to soft ball stage. Add sugar-syrup slowly to beaten egg whites and beat all thoroughly until icing is creamy. Now add the powdered sugar and blend.

CREAM CHEESE FROSTING

★

1 (3-ounce) package cream cheese

1 stick butter

1 (1-pound) box confectioners' sugar (3 cups unsifted)

1 teaspoon vanilla

1 cup pecans (optional)

Combine all ingredients except pecans. Beat until smooth and add pecans.

SMOOTH 'N CREAMY FROSTING

★

1 (3-ounce) box instant pudding and pie filling (any flavor)

¼ cup confectioners' sugar

1 cup cold milk

3½ cups or 1 (8-ounce) container Cool Whip

Combine pudding mix, sugar, and milk in a small bowl. Beat slowly with rotary beater or at lowest speed of electric mixer until well blended, about 1 minute. Fold in Cool Whip. Spread on cake at once. Store frosted cake in refrigerator. (MAKES ABOUT 4 CUPS, OR ENOUGH FOR TWO 9-INCH LAYERS)

PIÑA COLADA FROSTING

★

1 (8-ounce) package cream cheese, softened

1 (1-pound) box powdered sugar

1 teaspoon vanilla

1 (8-ounce) can crushed pineapple, drained well and blotted dry on paper towel (save a little juice)

Angel Flake sweetened coconut for sprinkling on top

Mix together cream cheese, powdered sugar, vanilla, and pineapple. Use 1 tablespoon pineapple juice if needed for the right consistency. Spread on cake and sprinkle with coconut.

CHOCOLATE FROSTING

★

2 cups unsifted powdered sugar

3 heaping teaspoons cocoa

1 teaspoon vanilla

2 to 3 tablespoons milk

Combine sugar, cocoa, vanilla, and enough milk to make of proper spreading consistency. Frost cake while hot for a shiny, smooth surface. Frosts 24 cupcakes or two 8-inch cake layers.

ROYAL ICING

(TO MAKE DECORATIONS)

★

6 teaspoons meringue powder

½ cup tap water

1½ pounds sifted powdered sugar

Beat meringue powder and water until stiff. Add powdered sugar. *This makes decorations that harden. If you want to use this icing for frosting your cake or making soft decorations, add 1 tablespoon cooking oil.*

CHEESECAKES, ICE CREAM, CANDIES, & OTHER DESSERTS

CHOCOLATE CHEESECAKE

★

1 cup graham cracker crumbs

¾ cup plus 3 tablespoons sugar

3 tablespoons margarine, melted

3 eggs

3 (3-ounce) packages cream cheese, softened

1¼ cups heavy cream

2 (4-ounce) bars sweet cooking chocolate

⅓ cup sifted flour

Pinch of baking soda

¼ teaspoon salt

1 teaspoon vanilla

Preheat oven to 325 degrees. ★ Combine graham cracker crumbs, 3 tablespoons of the sugar, and margarine. Sprinkle about ¼ cup crumb mixture around sides of a greased 9-inch springform pan. Press remainder to bottom of pan. ★ Beat eggs until fluffy and light in color. Add remaining ¾ cup sugar a little at a time, beating after each addition. Beat until well blended. Combine cream cheese and cream and beat until smooth and thick enough to mound. Melt chocolate and cool slightly. Blend into cream cheese. Fold in egg mixture. Sift together flour, baking soda, and salt. Stir into cheese mixture. Blend in vanilla. Turn into crumb-lined pan. Bake 1 hour and 5 minutes. Cool and serve with whipped cream if desired. (MAKES 16 SERVING)

EASY CHEESECAKE

★

CRUST

1 cup graham cracker crumbs

3 tablespoons sugar

3 tablespoons reduced-calorie margarine, melted

TOPPING

¾ cup sour cream

2 tablespoons sugar

½ teaspoon vanilla

FILLING

2 (8-ounce) packages light Philadelphia Brand Neufchâtel Cheese

⅓ cup sugar

2 eggs

1 teaspoon vanilla

Preheat oven to 350 degrees. Mix together crust ingredients; press into bottom and up sides of a 9-inch pie plate. Bake 10 minutes. ★ For filling, beat cheese and sugar together in large mixing bowl at medium speed with an electric mixer until well blended. Add eggs, one at a time, mixing well after each. Stir in vanilla; pour into crust. Bake 40 minutes. ★ Mix together topping ingredients. Spoon over warm cheesecake. Chill. Top with strawberries if desired. (MAKES 10 SERVING)

ICE CREAM DESSERT OR PIE

★

½ gallon deluxe vanilla ice cream, softened

½ cup fresh lemon juice (about 1 large or 2 small lemons)

1 cup sour cream

1 teaspoon vanilla

Grated rind of one lemon

Mix and refreeze all of the above. Serve in a dessert bowl with fruit of your choice as a topping—such as raspberries or strawberries. You can also put in a graham cracker crust and top with fruit. (MAKES 3 PIES)

BASIC ICE CREAM

★

1 envelope unflavored gelatin

¼ cup water

3 cups homogenized milk

5 eggs

2 cups sugar

2 (12-ounce) cans evaporated milk

1 teaspoon vanilla

1 teaspoon almond extract

Merest dash of salt

Soften gelatin in water. Heat one cup homogenized milk. Whir eggs, sugar, and one can evaporated milk in blender. Add hot milk to gelatin and stir until dissolved. Add to blender mixture. Add vanilla, almond extract, and salt and the rest of the milk. Pour all ingredients in ice cream freezer and stir until mixture is well blended. Freeze according to directions on your freezer.

> Additions you can make: Brandied Cherry—Stir 1 large can brandied cherries with juice into ice cream just before freezing. Brandied cherries are an imported item usually used for Cherries Jubilee and are available at specialty stores. ★ Crème de Menthe—Reduce homogenized milk in basic recipe to 2 cups and sugar to 1 cup. Stir in 1 cup crème de menthe. This is great with chocolate cake.

CHOCOLATE SAUCE
(FAMILY FAVORITE)

★

1½ cups sugar

1 cup cocoa

⅛ teaspoon salt

1 cup water

1 teaspoon vanilla

In a saucepan, mix sugar, cocoa, salt, and water. Place over medium heat. (Chocolate scorches easily; never use high heat.) Boil 15 minutes. Cool. Add vanilla. Use on ice cream, etc. Pour leftover sauce in a jar, cover, and refrigerate. Just warm the next time. (MAKES ABOUT 2 CUPS)

CHOCOLATE ICE CREAM

★

5 cups evaporated milk

1 cup sugar

2 squares (2 ounces) unsweetened
   baking chocolate, melted

1½ teaspoons vanilla

¼ teaspoon salt

Scald the milk. Dissolve sugar in 2 cups of the scalded milk. Pour sugar and milk mixture slowly over melted chocolate; stir constantly to avoid dark specks. Add the remaining 3 cups milk. Stir in vanilla and salt. Freeze according to ice cream freezer manufacturer's directions. This makes a much less expensive ice cream than most recipes because it depends on evaporated milk instead of cream or milk; it has fewer calories too. (MAKES 2 QUARTS)

CHOCOLATE TURTLES

★

½ pound soft caramels

2 tablespoons heavy cream

1 cup pecan halves or large,
   skinned, unsalted peanuts

4 squares Baker's semi-sweet
   chocolate

Melt caramels in cream over hot water; cool about 10 minutes. Place nuts on waxed paper in groups of three. Spoon caramel mixture over nuts, leaving tips showing. Let stand until set (about ½ hour). Meanwhile, melt chocolate over hot water; cool to lukewarm. Spread cooled chocolate over caramel.
(MAKES ABOUT 24)

DIVINITY
(GRANDMA POLASEK'S)

★

½ cup light corn syrup

2½ cups sugar

¼ teaspoon salt

½ cup water

2 egg whites

1 teaspoon vanilla

1 cup coarsely chopped pecans

Combine corn syrup, sugar, salt, and water in saucepan. Cook over medium heat, stirring constantly until sugar is dissolved. Cook, without stirring, to the firm ball stage (248 degrees) or until a small amount of syrup forms a firm ball which does not flatten when dropped into very cold water. Just before syrup reaches 248 degrees, beat egg whites with electric mixer until stiff but not dry. Pour about half the syrup slowly over egg whites, beating constantly. Cook the remainder of the syrup to the soft crack stage (272 degrees) or until a small amount of syrup separates into threads which are hard but not brittle when dropped into very cold water. Add syrup slowly to the first mixture, beating constantly. Continue beating until mixture holds its shape. If mixture becomes too heavy for beater, continue beating with a wooden spoon. Add vanilla and nuts. Drop from the tip of a spoon onto waxed paper. (MAKES ABOUT 1¼ POUNDS)

PEANUT BRITTLE

★

2 cups sugar

½ cup water

1 cup white corn syrup

2 cups raw peanuts

2 teaspoons baking soda

½ teaspoon salt

½ teaspoon vanilla

Combine sugar, water, and syrup in a saucepan. When mixture comes to a boil, add peanuts. Cook until it is an amber color. Remove from fire. Add baking soda, salt, and vanilla. Beat until well mixed. Pour on a well-buttered plate and let cool. (MAKES ABOUT 2 POUNDS)

COCONUT BALL BON-BONS

★

1 can sweetened condensed milk

2 (1-pound) boxes powdered sugar

2 cups shredded coconut

4 cups pecans, chopped

1 teaspoon vanilla

½ cup margarine

Pinch of salt

COATING

2 (4-ounce) packages German sweet
   chocolate bars

½ pound paraffin

Mix all Bon-Bon ingredients together, make into walnut size balls, and refrigerate overnight. ★ For coating: Melt chocolate and paraffin in a double boiler. Dip balls. (MAKES 70 BON-BONS)

EASY FUDGE

★

1⅔ cups sugar

⅛ teaspoon salt

1 (5-ounce) can evaporated milk

16 large marshmallows

1 (6-ounce) package semi-sweet
   chocolate pieces

1 teaspoon vanilla

½ cup chopped walnuts

In a heavy, 2-quart saucepan, combine sugar, salt, evaporated milk, and marshmallows. Cook, stirring, over medium heat to a full, all-over boil. Lower heat and keep stirring while mixture boils slowly for 5 minutes. Take off heat. Quickly add chocolate pieces and stir until chocolate is melted. Stir in vanilla and nuts. Pour into an 8 x 8 x 2-inch baking pan. Cool thoroughly. Cut into squares. (MAKES 36 PIECES)

PRALINES

★

2 cups sugar

1 cup firmly packed light brown
    sugar

¾ cup water

¼ cup light corn syrup

1 teaspoon vinegar

½ teaspoon salt

1 (6-ounce) package butterscotch
    morsels

¼ cup coarsely chopped walnuts or
    pecans

¼ cup hot water if needed

Combine sugars, water, corn syrup, vinegar, and salt in a 2-quart saucepan.
Bring to a full boil, stirring constantly. Boil over high heat 3 minutes; do not
stir. Remove from heat, add butterscotch morsels and heat until morsels are
melted. Mixture will be thin. Stir in nuts; drop by teaspoonfuls on ungreased
foil or heavy brown paper. If mixture becomes too thick, stir in small amount
of hot water. Chill or let stand at room temperature until set. (MAKES ABOUT 4
DOZEN)

MICROWAVE PRALINES

★

¾ cup buttermilk

2 cups sugar

2 cups pecan halves

½ teaspoon salt

2 tablespoons butter

1 teaspoon baking soda

Mix together buttermilk, sugar, pecans, salt, and butter in a 4- or 5-quart
microwave dish. Cook on high 12 minutes, stirring at 4-minute intervals. Stir in
baking soda until foamy. Cook on high 1 minute. (This last step gives the pralines
a caramel color). Beat mixture until tacky (about 1 minute). Drop by teaspoonfuls on a sheet of foil. (MAKES 20 PIECES)

DATE LOAF CANDY

★

2 cups sugar

1 cup milk

¼ cup butter

1 cup dates (or to taste), chopped

1 cup chopped nuts or shredded-coconut

1 teaspoon vanilla

Combine sugar, milk, and butter in a saucepan. Boil until a drop forms a hard ball when dropped into cold water. Add dates, nuts, and vanilla. Thoroughly wet a cloth and lay on counter. Pour the candy into a roll shape on the cloth and roll up in the cloth. Let sit overnight or until hard and cloth is dry. Unroll and slice. (MAKES 20-24 SLICES)

LEMON FREEZE

★

½ cup evaporated milk

1 egg, separated

⅓ cup sugar

3 tablespoons lemon juice

¼ teaspoon grated lemon rind

A few grains of salt

2 tablespoons graham cracker crumbs

Chill evaporated milk in ice tray until almost frozen at edges. Chill beaters for electric mixer. ★ In a 1-quart bowl mix egg yolk, sugar, 1 tablespoon of the lemon juice, lemon rind, and salt. Put ice-cold milk and egg white into cold small bowl of electric mixer. Using cold beaters, whip at high speed (or use) rotary beater until fluffy. Add remaining 2 tablespoons lemon juice and whip until stiff. Beat in sugar mixture gradually at low speed until well mixed. Put into 1-quart ice tray. Sprinkle graham cracker crumbs on top. Freeze until firm, about 1 hour. (SERVES 6)

RICE PUDDING

★

2 cups uncooked rice

4 cups cold water

2 tablespoons plus 1 teaspoon
  butter

½ teaspoon salt

¼ cup milk

2 eggs, beaten

¼ cup plus 3 tablespoons sugar plus
  some for sprinkling

2 tablespoons cinnamon

2 tablespoons butter

Cook rice in cold water along with 1 teaspoon of the butter and ½ teaspoon
salt. Bring to a boil and then cut heat down to your lowest setting for 15 minutes. Combine milk and eggs and add to rice. Add ¼ cup sugar. Mix all this and
place in baking dish. Sprinkle sugar and cinnamon on top and pat butter here
and there. Place in oven for 20 minutes at 350 degrees or put in microwave for
about 10 minutes. *(SERVES 6 TO 8 PEOPLE)*

CREAMY BANANA PUDDING

★

1 (14-ounce) can sweetened
  condensed milk

1½ cups cold water

1 (3-ounce) box instant vanilla
  pudding and pie filling mix

2 cups (1 pint) whipping cream,
  whipped

36 vanilla wafers

3 medium bananas, sliced and
  dipped in lemon juice

In a large bowl, combine milk and water and add pudding mix. Beat well. Chill
5 minutes. Fold in whipped cream. Spoon 1 cup pudding mixture into 2½-quart
glass serving bowl. Top with ⅓ each of the wafers, bananas, and pudding. Repeat
layering twice, ending with pudding. Chill thoroughly. Garnish as desired.
Refrigerate leftovers. *(SERVES 8 TO 10 PEOPLE)*

APPLE STRUDEL

★

1½ sticks margarine

1 cup warm milk

2 egg yolks

3 cups flour

Sugar and cinnamon for
sprinkling on filling

Nuts and raisins to taste (optional)

Your favorite fruit, such as apples or
pears, peeled and sliced with
potato peeler (enough to cover
rolled strudel dough)

Mix together margarine, milk, egg yolks, and flour and chill in refrigerator for at least 3 hours. Divide dough into 3 portions. Take one out to work with and place the two remaining ones into the refrigerator to keep cold. ★ Place one dough portion on a clean cloth on the table, sprinkle generously with flour, and roll it with a rolling pin as thin as possible. Brush the rolled-out dough with butter and spread with your favorite filling. If you want apples or pears, peel them and then start slicing away with potato peeler until the slices cover all the rolled-out dough. Sprinkle with sugar and cinnamon. Add nuts and raisins if desired. ★ Pick up cloth at one side, lift and roll slowly toward the other side (jelly roll style). Seal by pinching dough together. Pick up strudel carefully and place it on a greased baking pan. Brush top with butter. Bake about 40 minutes in a moderate oven at 350 degrees for about 45 minutes or until browned. This dough keeps well in the refrigerator for several days. (MAKES 15 1-INCH SLICES)

Agnes and Theo Polasek (in middle) on their 25th wedding anniversary, 1983.
With sisters, brothers and in-laws.

POKEY PUDDING

★

LAYER 1

1½ cups flour

1 stick butter, softened

¾ cup pecans

LAYER 2

1 (8-ounce) package cream cheese

1 pint Cool Whip

1½ cups powdered sugar

LAYER 3

1 (6-ounce) box chocolate instant pudding

1 (6-ounce) box vanilla instant pudding

3 cups milk

1 pint Cool Whip

1 Hershey's chocolate bar for garnish

Preheat oven to 350 degrees. ★ Place ingredients for layer 1 directly in a glass 13 x 9-inch baking dish, mix, and press into pan. Bake 30 minutes. ★ Mix together ingredients for layer 2 and spread on top. ★ Mix together ingredients for layer 3, spread on top, and then spread a layer of Cool Whip on top of that. Grate a Hershey's bar on top. (MAKES 24 SQUARES)

VANILLA PUDDING

★

⅓ cup sugar

¼ cup cornstarch

⅛ teaspoon salt

2¼ cups milk

2 tablespoons butter

1 teaspoon vanilla

Mix sugar, cornstarch, and salt. ★ Gradually stir in milk. Bring to a boil over medium heat, stirring constantly, and boil 1 minute. Remove from heat. Stir in butter and vanilla. Chill. (MAKES 2½ CUPS)

> For chocolate pudding increase sugar to ⅔ cup and add 3 tablespoons unsweetened cocoa mixed with cornstarch.

CHERRY WHIP
★

CRUST

2 cups crushed graham crackers

3 tablespoons powdered sugar

1 stick butter, softened

1 envelope unflavored gelatin

FILLING

1 large box Dream Whip

1 cup milk

1 teaspoon vanilla

1 cup sugar

1 (8-ounce) package cream cheese, softened

2 cans cherry pie filling

Mix graham cracker crumbs and powdered sugar together and add butter. Press into 9 x 13-inch pan. Sprinkle gelatin over top. ★ Mix together Dream Whip, milk, and vanilla until stiff and then add sugar and the softened cream cheese. Pour into crust. Pour 2 cans of cherry pie mix on top. Chill. (MAKES 18 SERVINGS)

APPLE CRUNCH
★

8 medium-size apples, cut into quarters and then thin slices

1 teaspoon cinnamon

1 teaspoon nutmeg

½ cup sugar

½ cup water

1 cup sifted flour

½ cup brown sugar

½ cup butter

½ cup chopped pecans

Preheat oven to 400 degrees. ★ Put apples in lightly buttered baking dish. Sprinkle cinnamon, nutmeg, and sugar over apple slices. Add water. Mix flour with brown sugar in a small bowl. Add butter. Mix well using pastry blender. Add chopped pecans. Spread mixture over apples. Place in oven for 20 minutes. Then turn heat down to 350 degrees for 25 minutes longer. (MAKES 8 SERVINGS)

PEANUT BUTTER BANANA MUFFINS
★

1 cup flour

¾ cup Quaker oats

½ cup firmly packed brown sugar

1 tablespoon baking powder

1 cup milk

½ cup peanut butter

½ cup mashed banana

1 egg, beaten

2 tablespoons corn oil

1 teaspoon vanilla

TOPPING

¼ cup uncooked oats

¼ cup flour

2 tablespoons butter

2 tablespoons brown sugar

Preheat oven at 350 degrees. ★ Combine flour, oats, brown sugar, and baking powder. Whisk together milk, peanut butter, banana, egg, oil, and vanilla and add to mixture. Fill muffins cups ¾ full. Bake 16 to 18 minutes or until golden brown. ★ Mix topping ingredients together and top warm muffins.
(MAKES 12 MUFFINS)

PECAN CLUSTERS
★

¼ cup butter

½ cup sugar

1 teaspoon vanilla

1½ squares unsweetened
    chocolate, melted

1 egg

½ cup flour

¼ teaspoon baking powder

2 cups pecans

Preheat oven to 350 degrees. ★ Combine all ingredients except pecans. Mix well and add pecans. Drop by teaspoonfuls onto a cookie sheet. Bake 10 minutes.
(MAKES ABOUT 12 SERVINGS)

ÉCLAIRS

★

½ cup butter

1 cup boiling water

1 cup sifted flour

¼ teaspoon salt

4 eggs

CUSTARD FILLING

3 tablespoons cornstarch

⅓ cup sugar

⅛ teaspoon salt

½ cup cold milk

1½ cups scalded milk

1 teaspoon vanilla

2 egg yolks beaten with 2 tablespoons milk

Preheat oven to 450 degrees. ★ Melt butter in saucepan over boiling water. Add flour and salt all at one time. Stir vigorously. Cook, stirring constantly, until the mixture forms a ball that doesn't separate. Remove from heat and cool slightly. Add eggs one at a time, beating hard after each addition, until mixture is smooth. ★ Insert a number 32 tip in cookie press, fill with mixture, and form éclair 1 inch wide and 3 to 4 inches long. Bake for 15 minutes, turn heat down to 325 degrees and bake for 25 minutes. Fill with custard when cool ★ Scald milk and then add all other ingredients. Cook over medium heat until thick. Slice éclairs lengthwise but not totally open and fill with custard. (MAKES 6 TO 8 SERVINGS)

FRESH FRUIT DIP

★

1 (8-ounce) package Philadelphia
cream cheese, softened

1 (7-ounce) jar Kraft
marshmallow créme

Combine cream cheese and marshmallow créme; mix well until blended. Serve with fresh fruit and cookies as dippers. (MAKES 2 CUPS)

Variation: Add 1 tablespoon orange juice and 1 teaspoon grated orange rind to mixture. May be served as a sauce over fresh fruit or shortcake.

BEVERAGES

★

Theo and Agnes Polasek, 1991.

CAMPER'S CHOCOLATE

★

1 (25-ounce) box instant milk   *1 (15-ounce) box Nestle's Quick*

1 (22-ounce) box Creamora   *1 (1-pound) box powdered Sugar*

Shake all ingredients together and store in airtight container. Dissolve by tea-spoonfuls in a glass of milk according to taste. Store in airtight container.
(MAKES ABOUT 3 QUARTS OF POWDERED CHOCOLATE MIXTURE)

SPICE TEA

★

2 cups Tang   *1 teaspoon cinnamon*

½ cup instant tea with lemon and   *½ teaspoon cloves*
    sweetening

Mix all ingredients together
in a jar and shake up. Mix
two teaspoons per cup of
hot water.

*Theo & Agnes Polasek, fishing on
the San Bernard River, 1988.*

CHOCOLATE SHAKE

★

½ cup nonfat dry milk

¼ cup water

3 tablespoons chocolate-
flavored syrup

1 cup ice cubes

Place all ingredients in a blender and blend until all ice is crushed.
(MAKES 1¼ CUPS)

STRAWBERRY SHAKE

★

1½ cups fresh or frozen unsweetened strawberries, thawed

⅓ cup nonfat dry milk

¼ cup plain yogurt

1 or 2 tablespoons honey

½ teaspoon vanilla

½ cup ice cubes

Place all ingredients in blender and blend until all ice is crushed.
(MAKES 2 CUPS)

ORANGE SHAKE

★

1 cup orange juice

⅓ cup nonfat dry milk

1 to 2 tablespoons sugar

½ teaspoon vanilla

½ cup ice cubes

Place all ingredients in a blender and blend until all ice cubes are crushed.
(MAKES 2 CUPS)

SLUSH PUNCH

★

3 (0.15-ounce) packets Kool-Aid (no sugar)

1 teaspoon vanilla

1 teaspoon almond extract

3 cups sugar

1 (46-ounce) can pineapple juice

2 (46-ounce) cans water

1 lemon, sliced

Three cans Fresca, Sprite, or 7-Up

Combine Kool-Aid, vanilla, almond extract, sugar, pineapple juice, and water, and freeze to slush. When serving add lemon slices and soda. *(MAKES ABOUT 20 QUARTS)*

LUSH SLUSH

★

1 (8-ounce) can crushed pineapple

2 bananas, mashed

1 cup sugar

1 (6-ounce) can frozen orange juice concentrate

2 cups cold ginger ale

Blend all ingredients in a blender and freeze until slushy. *(SERVES 6)*

EASY PARTY PUNCH

★

1 quart unsweetened pineapple juice, chilled

1 quart orange juice, chilled

1 quart apple juice, chilled

2 quarts ginger ale, chilled

2 quarts lime sherbet

Chill juices and ginger ale. Pour into a punch bowl. Top with scoops of sherbet. *(MAKES 50 SERVINGS)*

WASSAIL BOWL

★

1 quart apple cider

1 cup orange juice

¾ cup lemon juice

½ cup sugar

1 teaspoon whole allspice

1 teaspoon whole cloves

3 cinnamon sticks

Combine juices with sugar and spices in a large pot. Bring to a simmer, strain, and serve hot. A delightful Christmas drink to serve to friends and family. *(YIELDS 16 HALF-CUP SERVINGS)*

Agnes and Logene Foster's grandchildren Alexandra, Chandler, Cole, and Georgia, 1998.

CHAMPAGNE PUNCH

★

1 bottle champagne (André or Jacques Bonet)	1 jigger (1-½ ounces) Orange Curacao
1 quart ginger ale	Ice ring containing strawberries and orange slices

Chill champagne, ginger ale, and Curacao. Place ice ring in a punch bowl and pour liquids over it. *(MAKES 79 OUNCES)*

Lynn Foster's wedding, 1993. From left: Lonnie, Agnes, Lynn, Logene, Larry.

PICKLES &
CANNING

★

Agnes and Logene Foster, 1993.

DILL PICKLE RECIPE
(MOTHER'S)

★

8 cups water	4 or 5 onions, sliced
4 cups sugar	1 bunch celery, cut into sticks
4 tablespoons salt	Small hot peppers, sliced (optional)
3 cups 9-grain vinegar	Several garlic cloves, sliced
Some fresh dill (about 4 cups—1 cup per quart of pickles)	2 bunches carrots, cut into sticks
	Cucumbers (as many as you like)

The first thing you do is wash pickles. We used to wash by hand (as we all remember). Now Mother places pickles in washing machine on cold water cycle along with a lot of towels on the bottom, sides, and between cucumbers so they won't get bruised. ★ What Mother and I do is: She starts the liquid (water, sugar, salt, and vinegar) in a large pot, depending on how many pickles you are putting up. Usually we do half a bushel of cucumbers at a time (above ingredients are for half a bushel). She lets that start to boil and as all this is happening, I start cutting up all of the above sliced ingredients and washing the dill. ★ Then I start stuffing jars with pickles, the larger ones at the bottom and finishing out with smaller ones at top. Put some dill in bottom of jar before you start stuffing. Place carrots and celery sticks alongside pickles. This is mostly for color and they are good pickled. Also put more dill on top along with sliced onion, garlic, and pepper (optional). When the liquid boils, start pouring it into filled pickle jars. Leave about 3/4-inch at top of each jar without liquid. Cap with new lids and new rings. Always use new lids. Hand-tighten. Use cold-pack canning method. (Use large, cold-pack canning pot and place jars in metal rack in pot. If you don't have a rack in your canner or pot, use towels. We use a very large pot and put a towel in the bottom and in between jars.) Fill canner with jars and then put in water almost to top of jars. Cook on medium heat. Slowly cook until pickles start to change color. Take out and set aside to cool. Make sure lids are tight.

You can use this same method for putting up sliced pickles, except you cook the sliced pickles before packing in jars. ★ *You can use this same method for putting up okra: use ½ cup sugar and 1 cup vinegar.*

BREAD-AND-BUTTER PICKLES

★

Cucumbers (as many as you like)

1 cup sugar

1 cup water

1 cup vinegar (if using 9-grain use only ½ cup)

1 tablespoon salt

Dash of turmeric

Fresh dill (about 1 cup fresh dill per quart)

1 onion, sliced rather fine

Wash cucumbers and slice as desired. Bring sugar, water, vinegar, salt, and turmeric to a boil. Then put cucumbers and onion in and boil until cucumbers turn color. Put ½ cup dill in bottom of jar and fill with cooked cucumbers and onion. Put ½ cup dill on top. Seal with lid and jar ring. Tighten. You can double or triple, or whatever you like. (MAKES 1 QUART)

SUNSHINE PICKLES

★

Medium or large cucumbers to fill 1-quart jar

1 tablespoon canning salt

Fresh dill (about 1 cup per quart of cucumbers)

1 teaspoon 9-grain vinegar

Wash cucumbers. Place dill in bottom of a 1-quart jar. Pack cucumbers in jar and add canning salt and vinegar. Put more dill on top and fill jar with water. Leave a little room right at the top. Put on new lid and ring and tighten. Place outside in the sun until they change color, about 1 week. Refrigerate after opening. ★ You can also put really large cucumbers in a gallon jar. Quadruple the ingredients. Put dill on the bottom, then cucumbers, salt, and vinegar. Put more dill on top and fill with water. Leave some room at top. Seal with lid and ring and tighten.

EASY AND GREAT SWEET PICKLES

★

1 gallon sour whole pickles　　　　　1 (5-pound) bag of sugar

Pour juice off of pickles and dump pickles into bowl. Slice pickles and put them back in jar. Halfway through, add half of the sugar. Continue slicing the rest of the pickles and then cover with sugar. Keep in pantry or refrigerator. Takes about 3 weeks before ready to eat.

SOUR PICKLES

★

Cucumbers to fill 1-quart jar

1 teaspoon allspice

Fresh dill (about 1 cup per quart of pickles)

4 tablespoons salt

8 tablespoons sugar

2 cups 9-grain vinegar

1 cup water

¼ teaspoon garlic powder or 1 clove fresh garlic

Wash cucumbers. Mix remaining ingredients together (do not boil liquid). Just pour over pickles packed in jars, then put in cold pack canner (Dill Pickle Recipe, page 132). Bring to a slow boil until the pickles change in color slightly, then remove from hot water; set aside to cool.

PICKLED CUCUMBERS 1

★

Cucumbers to fill 1-quart jar

1 teaspoon allspice

Fresh dill (about 1 cup per quart of
   pickles)

4 tablespoons salt

8 tablespoons sugar

2 cups 9-grain vinegar

1 cup water

¼ teaspoon garlic powder or 1 clove
   fresh garlic

Wash cucumbers. Mix remaining ingredients together (do not boil liquid). Just
pour over pickles packed in jars, then put in cold pack canner (Dill Pickle
Recipe, page 132). Bring to a slow boil until the pickles change in color slightly,
then remove from hot water; set aside to cool.

PICKLED CUCUMBERS 2

★

Cucumbers to fill 1-quart jar

Fresh dill (about 1 cup per quart of
   pickles)

1 garlic clove

⅓ cup sugar

⅓ cup 9-grain vinegar

1 tablespoon salt

Dash of turmeric

Wash cucumbers. Place ½ cup dill in bottom of jar, then cucumbers, then garlic, sugar, vinegar, salt, and turmeric. Then put ½ cup dill on top. Fill to within
½ inch of top of jar with cold tap water. Use cold-pack canning method (see
Dill Pickle Recipe, page 132).

Four generations: Agnes Foster, Agnes Polasek holding Georgia Foster, and Lynn Foster, 1995.

OKRA JUMBO
★

6 cups okra, sliced

2 cups (about 2 medium) squash, chopped or sliced

1 cup celery, chopped

½ cup chopped onion

3 cups chopped tomatoes

½ teaspoon pepper

2 tablespoons sugar

5 tablespoons vinegar

Salt to taste

Put all ingredients in a pot and cook slowly 20 minutes or until vegetables are soft; pack in pint jars and pressure cook 35 minutes at 10 pounds pressure.

SHELLED FRESH BLACK-EYED PEAS
★

Wash and shell enough black-eyed peas to fill as many pint jars as you like. Pour into clean, hot glass jars. Fill pints to 1½ inches from rim and quarts to 2 inches from rim. Do not push or shake down peas (to do so would increase the amount of peas in the jar and give a poor fill). Cover the peas with fresh, boiling water and work out the bubbles with a knife blade. Add more water to ½ inch from the top of the jar and add ½ teaspoon salt to each jar. Wipe the top of the jar with a clean, damp cloth. Close with 2-piece self-sealing closures. Place in hot pressure cooker. Process at 10 pounds pressure. Pint jar: 35 minutes. Quart jar: 40 minutes.

RED BEETS
★

2 cups water

1 cup sugar

1 cup vinegar

1 quart cooked and sliced red beets

Put all ingredients in a saucepan and bring to a boil. Cook ten minutes. Put in jars. Pour liquid in jar and seal with tight lid and ring.

FRESH LIMA BEANS

★

Use only young, tender beans. Shell and wash enough lima beans to fill as many jars as you like without precooking. Pour beans into clean jars to 1 inch from top of jar for pints and 1½ inches for quarts for the small-bean type. For the large beans of the "baby potato" type, fill to ¾ inch from top for pints and 1¼ inches for quarts. Beans should be raked level with fork before measuring, but should not be pushed or shaken down (to do so would increase the amount of beans in the jar and give a poor fill). Add ½ teaspoon salt to pints and 1 teaspoon to quarts. Fill jar level full with boiling water. Close with 2-piece self-sealing closures, being careful that no food particles remain on top of jar to cause a poor seal. Process in pressure cooker at 10 pounds pressure. Pint jar: 40 minutes. Quart jar: 50 minutes .

Grandma Polasek and family, 1996.

Joe, Mary, Logene, Agnes F., Emily, John, Mary Ann, Theo L., Agnes and Theo Polasek.

Joe Jr. and Jennifer Polasek, 1998.

COOKING TIPS

★

Polasek Family, 1995.

ROASTING

Cut	Weight Range	Cooking Temperature	Internal Meat Temperature	Approximate Time
BEEF				
Standing Ribs (3)	6–8 lbs.	325*		
Rare			140	16–18 min. per lb.
Medium			160	20–22 min. per lb.
Well Done			170	25–30 min. per lb.
Rolled Rib	5–7 lbs.	325		Add 10 to 12 min. per lb. to above time
Rump, boneless	5–7 lbs.	325	170	30 min. per lb.
LAMB				
Leg	6–7 lbs.	325	175–180	30–35 min. per lb.
Shoulder (bone in)	5–7 lbs.	325	175–180	30–35 min. per lb.
Shoulder (boneless roll)	4–6 lbs.	325	175–180	40–45 min. per lb.
FRESH PORK				
Loin	4–5 lbs.	350	185	30–35 min. per lb.
Cushion Shoulder	4–6 lbs.	350	185	35–40 min. per lb.
Shoulder (boned & rolled)	4–6 lbs.	350	185	40–45 min. per lb.
Shoulder (butt)	4–6 lbs.	350	185	45–50 min. per lb.
Fresh Ham	10–14 lbs.	350	185	30–35 min. per lb.
Spare Ribs (1 side)	1½–2½ lbs.	350	185	1–1½ hrs. total
SMOKED PORK				
Ham—whole	10–12 lbs.	325	150	18–20 min. per lb.
	14–16 lbs.	325	150	16–18 min. per lb.
Ham–half	6–8 lbs.	325	150	25–27 min. per lb.
Ham–2-inch slice	2½–3 lbs.	325	170	1½ hrs. total
Picnic	5–8 lbs.	325	170	33–35 min. per lb.
POULTRY				
Chickens				
Stuffed weight	4–5 lbs.	325	185	35–40 min. per lb.
	over 5 lbs.	325	185	20–25 min. per lb.
Turkeys				
Stuffed weight	6–10 lbs.	325	185	20–25 min. per lb.
	10–16 lbs.	325	185	18–20 min. per lb.
	18–25 lbs.	325	185	15–18 min. per lb.

Geese—Same as turkey of similar weight

Duck—Same as heavy chicken of similar weight

All temperatures refer to degrees Fahrenheit.

BROILING

Cut	Thickness	Weight	Approximate Total Time (minutes)		
			Rare	Medium	Well Done
BEEF					
Rib Steak	1 inch	1–1½ lbs.	8–10	12–14	18–20
Club Steak	1 inch	1–1½ lbs.	8–10	12–14	18–20
Porterhouse	1 inch	1½–2 lbs.	10–12	14–16	20–25
	2 inch	3–3½ lbs.	20–25	30–35	40–45
Sirloin	1 inch	2½–3½ lbs.	10–12	14–16	20–25
	1½ inch	3½–4½ lbs.	14–16	18–20	25–30
	2 inch	5–5½ lbs.	20–25	30–35	40–45
Ground Beef Patties	¾ inch	4 oz. ea.	8	12	15
Tenderloin	1 inch	6–8 ounces	8–10	12–14	18–20
LAMB					
Rib or Loin					
Chops (1 rib)	¾ inch	2–3 oz.			14–15
Double Rib	1½ inch	4–5 oz. ea.			22–25
Lamb Shoulder					
Chops	¾ inch	3–4 oz. ea.			14–15
	1½ inch	5–6 oz. ea.			22–25
Lamb Patties	¾ inch	4 oz. each			14–15
HAM, BACON &					
SAUSAGE					
Ham Slices	½ inch	9–12 oz. ea.			10–12
	¾ inch	1–1¼ lb.			13–14
	1 inch	1¼–1¾ lbs.			18–20
Bacon					4–5
Pork Sausage Links		12–16 to the lb.			12–15
Broiling Chickens					
(drawn) halves		1–1½ lbs.			30–35

STEWING

Cut	Weight Range	Approximate Time
Beef–1½-inch cubes from neck, chuck, plate or heel of round	2 lbs.	2½–3 hrs.
Veal or Lamb—1–1½-inch cubes from shoulder or breast	2 lbs.	1½–3 hrs.
Chicken	3½–4 lbs.	2–2½ hrs.

BRAISING

Cut	Weight	Approximate Time*
Beef Pot Roast, Chuck, Rump, or Heel of Round	3–5 lbs	3½–4 hrs.
Swiss Steak, round (1 inch thick)	2 lbs.	1½–2 hrs.
Flank Steak	1½–2 lbs	1½ hrs.
Beef Short Ribs	2–2½ lbs.	2–2½ hrs.
Ox Tails	1–1½ lbs.	3–4 hrs.
Rolled Lamb Shoulder Pot Roast	3–5 lbs.	2–2½ hrs.
Lamb Shoulder Chops	4–5 lbs.	35–40 min.
Lamb Neck Slices	½ lb. each	1–1½ hrs.
Lamb Shanks	1 lb. each	1½ hrs.
Pork Rib or Loin Chops	4–5 oz. each (¾ to 1 inch)	35–40 min.
Pork Shoulder Steaks	5–6 oz. each	35–40 min.
Veal Rolled Shoulder Pot Roast	4–5½ lbs	2–2½ hrs.
Cutlets or Round	2 lbs.	45–50 min.
Loin or Rib Chops	3–5 oz. each	45–50 min.

Brown all meats before simmering for the specified time.

MEASUREMENT CONVERSIONS

A pinch ....⅛ teaspoon or less

3 teaspoons ....1 tablespoon

4 tablespoons ....¼ cup

8 tablespoons ....½ cup

12 tablespoons ....¾ cup

16 tablespoons ....1 cup

2 cups...1 pint

4 cups...1 quart

4 quarts...1 gallon

8 quarts...1 peck

4 pecks...1 bushel

16 ounces...1 pound

32 ounces...1 quart

8 ounces liquid...1 cup

1 ounce liquid...2 tablespoons

Make all measurements level.

HELPFUL COOKING HINTS

- Let a roast stand for at least an hour at room temperature before you begin to cook. Before baking and during baking brush with oil (this helps seal in the juices). Roasts with bone in will cook faster than a boneless roast: the bone carries the heat to the inside of the roast faster. If you oversalt the gravy, just add some instant mashed potatoes. You will probably need to add some more water to get the right consistency to the gravy.
- When slicing raw meat into thin strips, partially freeze first. It will slice easier.
- When freezing meatballs, place them on a cookie sheet until they are frozen. Then place in plastic bags.
- Add sugar to the water instead of salt when boiling corn. Salt toughens the corn.
- To ripen tomatoes faster, put them in a brown paper bag in a dark pantry and they will ripen overnight. Also place the tomatoes on your window sill in the sunlight until they ripen rather than putting them in refrigerator immediately. After they are ripened, then place in refrigerator.
- Buy mushrooms before they "open." They are truly fresh when stems and caps are attached.
- When cooking cabbage, place a small tin cup or can half full of vinegar on the stove near the cabbage to absorb the odors.
- For crispier french fries, let raw potatoes stand in cold water for at least half an hour before frying.
- Always use a wood, glass, or china bowl when mixing your salad.
- Do not wash lettuce when you bring it home from the store. Place it just as it is in refrigerator without washing. Wash the day you are going to use.
- To keep celery crisp, place it standing up in a pitcher of cold, salted water and re-frigerate.

COOKING TERMS

AU GRATIN: A dish cooked with a layer of crumbs and/or cheese to make a browned crust.

AU JUS: Served in its own juices.

BASTE: To drip or pour pan drippings or melted butter on meat while cooking so that it will not dry out.

BISQUE: A rich, thick cream soup.

BLANCH: To boil briefly and then chill.

CREAM: To make into a smooth mixture like cream, such as beating butter and sugar until creamy.

CRIMP: To pinch the edges of the dough of a two-crust pie at intervals with the fingers or by pressing the two pie crusts together with the tines of a fork, making a wavy edge.

DREDGE: To coat lightly with flour, etc.

ENTRÉE: The main dish of food.

FOLD: To add to a mixture by gently turning one part over another with strokes of a spoon (such as folding beaten eggs into another mixture).

JULIENNE: To cut into thin strips.

MARINATE: To allow food to stand in a liquid to tenderize or to add flavor.

MEUNIERE: To dredge with flour and then sauté in butter.

MINCE: To cut up or chop into very small pieces or to shred.

PARBOIL: To boil until partly cooked.

PARE: To shave the outer part off of something such as taking off the skin of fruit.

POACH: To cook by breaking food such as fish into water that is simmering.

PURÉE: To boil until soft and then push through a sieve.

SAUTÉ: To cook or brown in a little oil.

SCALD: To heat almost to the boiling point, but not quite.

SIMMER: To cook something at or just below the boiling point.

SUBSTITUTIONS

Ingredient	Quantity	Substitute
Self-rising flour	1 cup	1 cup all-purpose flour, ½ teaspoon salt, and 1 teaspoon baking powder
Cornstarch	1 tablespoon	2 tablespoons flour or 2 teaspoons quick-cooking tapioca
Baking powder	1 teaspoon	¼ teaspoon baking soda plus ½ teaspoon cream of tartar
Powdered sugar	1 cup	1 cup granulated sugar plus 1 teaspoon cornstarch
Brown sugar	½ cup	2 tablespoons molasses in ½ cup granulated sugar
Sour milk	1 cup	1 tablespoon lemon juice or vinegar plus sweet milk to make 1 cup (let stand 5 min.)
Whole milk	1 cup	½ cup evaporated milk plus ½ cup water
Cracker crumbs	¾ cup	1 cup bread crumbs
Chocolate	1 square (1 oz.)	3 or 4 tablespoon cocoa plus 1 tablespoon butter*
Fresh herbs	1 tablespoon	1 teaspoon dried herbs
Fresh onion	1 small	1 tablespoon instant minced onion, rehydrated
Dry Mustard	1 teaspoon	1 tablespoon prepared mustard
Tomato juice	1 cup	½ cup tomato sauce plus ½ cup water
Catsup or chili sauce	1 cup	1 cup tomato sauce plus ½ cup sugar and 2 tablespoon vinegar (for use in cooking).
Dates	1 lb	1½ cups dates, pitted and cut
Bananas	3 medium	1 cup mashed
Miniature marshmallows	10	1 large marshmallow

NOTE: Brown and white sugars can be used interchangeably.

You must reduce the amount of flour when substituting cocoa for chocolate in cakes.

TIME TABLE FOR COOKING VEGETABLES

Vegetable	Cooking Method	Cooking Time (minutes)
Asparagus Tips	Boiled	10–15
Artichokes, French	Boiled	40
	Steamed	45–60
Beans, Lima	Boiled	20–40
	Steamed	60
Beans, String	Boiled	15–35
	Steamed	60
Beets, young with skin	Boiled	30
	Steamed	60
	Baked	70–90
Beets, old	Boiled or Steamed	60–120
Broccoli, flowerets	Boiled	5–10
Broccoli, stems	Boiled	20–30
Brussels Sprouts	Boiled	20–30
Cabbage, chopped	Boiled	10–20
	Steamed	25
Cauliflower, stem down	Boiled	20–30
Cauliflower, flowerets	Boiled	8–10
Carrots, cut across	Boiled	8–10
	Steamed	40
Corn, tender	Boiled	5–10
	Steamed	15
	Baked	20
Corn on the cob	Boiled	8–10
	Steamed	15
Eggplant, whole	Boiled	30
	Steamed	40
	Baked	45
Parsnips	Boiled	25–40
	Steamed	60
	Baked	60–75
Peas, green	Boiled	5–15
	Steamed	5–15
Potatoes	Boiled	20–40
	Steamed	60
	Baked	45–60
Pumpkin or Squash	Boiled	20–40
	Steamed	45
	Baked	60
Tomatoes	Boiled	5–15
Turnips	Boiled	25–40

HINTS FOR MAKING PERFECT DESSERTS

COOKIES:

• Refrigerate your dough for at least 20 to 30 minutes if you plan to roll dough out. If not refrigerated, the soft dough may require more flour. Too much flour makes cookies hard and brittle.

• To roll out dough, place on a floured board. Flour the rolling pin slightly and roll lightly to desire thickness.

• To bake, put cookie sheets in upper third of oven. You have to really watch cookies carefully while baking . Never leave the room or you will probably ruin that batch. The ten minutes really pass fast.

PIES AND CAKES:

• Always cool your pie crust ingredients before starting.

• The lower crust should be flat. Prick with a fork and make sure there are no bubbles underneath.

• Sprinkle crust with powdered sugar to avoid a soggy crust when making custard pies.

• When making meringue, beat egg whites until you can turn the bowl over without spilling them. Add ½ teaspoon cornstarch and beat in and you are ready to put on pie.

• When making a cake, fill cake pans about ⅔ full and spread batter well into corners and to the sides.

• Time your cake carefully. When the time is up, place a toothpick in the middle: If it comes out clean, the cake is done.

• Place cake on a rack for about five minutes when you take it out of the oven. Then loosen the sides and the turn cake out on rack to finish cooling.

• Cool cakes thoroughly before frosting unless the recipe states otherwise.

QUANTITIES TO SERVE 25 TO 100 PEOPLE

Food	25 people	50 people	100 people
SANDWICHES			
Bread	50 slices or 3 (1-pound) loaves	100 slices or 6 (1-pound) loaves	200 slices or 12 (1-pound) loaves
Mayonnaise or Mustard	1½ cups	3 cups	6 cups
Mixed Filling (meat, eggs, fish)	1½ quarts	3 quarts	6 quarts
Lettuce	1½ heads	3 heads	6 heads
MEAT, POULTRY, AND FISH			
Wieners	6½ pounds	13 pounds	26 pounds
Hamburger	9 pounds	18 pounds	36 pounds
Turkey or Chicken	13 pounds	25 to 35 pounds	50 to 75 pounds
Fish fillets or steak	7½ pounds	15 pounds	30 pounds
SALADS AND SIDE DISHES			
Potato Salad	4½ quarts	2¼ gallons	4½ gallons
Scalloped Potatoes	4½ quarts	9 quarts	18 quarts
Spaghetti	1¼ gallons	2½ gallons	5 gallons
Baked Beans	¾ gallon	1½ gallons	3 gallons
Jell-O Salad	¾ gallon	1½ gallons	3 gallons
Nuts	1 pound	2 pounds	4 pounds
Olives	¾ pound	1½ pounds	3 pounds
BEVERAGES			
Coffee	½ pound and 1½ gallons water	1 pound and 3 gallons water	2 pounds and 6 gallons water
Tea	$\frac{1}{12}$ pound and 1½ gallons water	⅙ pound and 3 gallons water	⅓ pound and 6 gallons water
Lemonade	10 to 15 lemons and 1½ gallons water	20 to 30 lemons and 3 gallons water	40 to 60 lemons and 6 gallons
Water			
DESERTS			
Watermelon	37½ pounds	75 pounds	150 pounds
Cake	one 10 x 12-inch sheet cake	one 12 x 20-inch sheet cake	two 12 x 20-inch sheet cakes
	one 10-inch layer cake	three 10-inch layer cakes	six 10-inch layer cakes
Whipping Cream	¾ pint	1½ to 2 pints	3 pints
Ice Cream	2¼ quarts	4½ quarts	9 quarts

INDEX

Note: italic page numbers indicate pictures.

★

✂⋆✿⋆✂

AGNES FOSTER is the mother of three boys and has four grand-children. She grew up in Wharton, Texas, until 1959 when she married Logene Foster and moved to Fort Bend County where they have lived ever since. Agnes is the bookkeeper for the Foster Law Firm as well as the bookkeeper and co-owner of L & A Racing.

AGNES POLASEK is the mother of four children. She has twelve grandchildren and sixteen great-grandchildren. She has lived in Wharton, Texas, most of her life and was married to Theo Otto Polasek for sixty-two years. Agnes operated a burger stand at her house for school children, called The Little Inn, for 20 years.